Leadership
Management
Administratorship

From A to Z Concepts about
Leadership and Management

Aybars Öztuna

FriesenPress

Suite 300 - 990 Fort St
Victoria, BC, V8V 3K2
Canada

www.friesenpress.com

Copyright © 2016 by Aybars Öztuna
First Edition — 2016

ISBN
978-1-5255-0086-2 (Hardcover)
978-1-5255-0087-9 (Paperback)
978-1-5255-0088-6 (eBook)

1. SELF-HELP, COMMUNICATION & SOCIAL SKILLS

Distributed to the trade by The Ingram Book Company

To: ~~Mr.~~ ~~████~~ ~~████~~ Rosse

FROM: Aybars Öztuna

With regards.

A. Öztuna

27th March 2017

Table of Contents

Foreword   xi

Leadership and Life Management in Family   1

Alternate Paths   3

Analytical and Holistic Thinking   5

Leadership in Knowledge Acquisition   7

Knowledge Management   9

Individual Leadership-Administratorship-Management   11

Managing Diversity   14

Being Focused on Solutions   17

Consultant   19

Managing Change   20

Assuring Balance   23

Dynamism   24

Disciplinary   25

Intellectual Leadership / Management /
Administratorship   28

Depressors   30

Team Leadership   32

Critical Leadership   35

Effective Leadership   37

Developmental Leadership / Management / Administratorship   39

Assignment   41

Visual Angle   42

Leadership in Our Daily Lives   44

Culture in Our Daily Lives   46

Trust, Trustworthiness   48

Dominance   50

Harmonic Management   53

Mistakes   54

Leadership in Animals   55

Persuasive Skill   57

Foresight   61

Communication in Leadership and Administration   63

First Impression   65

Human Management   68

Initiative   70

Stability   72

Practicalness   75

Business Life and Private Life   77

Reputation Management   80

Acceptance Policy   82

Permanence   84

Open Door and Closed Door Policies   85

Steering Your Career   88

Charisma   91

Concept - Word   93

Gain   94

Coach   97

Condition   99

Coordination   101

Crisis Management   103

Leadership Steps   108

Leadership and Politics   111

Satisfaction   113

Mission   115

Self-Control   117

Point Shot   119

Our Priorities   121

Self-Management   122

Plan   124

Uncovering the Potential and Managing
the Potential Change   125

Project Management   128

Radical Leadership 130

Risk Taking 131

Spiritual Leadership 133

Health Management 135

Leadership of Virtual Teams 137

Leadership in the Art and Art Management 140

Respect, Dignity 142

Love, Value 145

Intuitive Leadership 148

Classroom Management 150

Abstract and Concrete Leadership Concepts 152

Leadership in Sport 153

Strategic Thinking 155

Continuity 157

Luck 158

Chief 160

Being Watchdog 162

Imitation 163

Style 165

Technology Management 167

Meeting Management 169

Conformance 173

Managing Your Superior   175

Yield Management   179

Vision   181

Creativity Management   183

Motivation in Our Lives   185

Stress in Our Lives   187

Competition in Our Lives   189

Being a New Manager   192

Talent Management   194

Authority   196

Authorization Competence   197

Mentor   198

Steps of Administratorship   199

Management Systems   201

Governance   202

Superficiality and Profundity   203

Leadership in Time and Time Management   205

Timing   207

Epilogue   208

Aybars Öztuna   209

"A leader who has understood the management approach, and has expressed it with short and effective expressions, he is Aybars Öztuna. Book is very important and valuable in terms of readability, management and addressing the important points of life."

Sinan Kızıldağ

Vodafone Vice Chairman of Executive Board

"Today, while most of the youngsters spend their time with internet and mobile phones, I congratulate Aybars Öztuna on his virtuous stance of authorship and his great mastery of the topics in this book. Nowadays, there are a few authors who successfully write about this issue. I have read some books that have put down prospective ideas on paper. The author of this book will gain good support in the future as this book shows that clearly. I wish his success will continuously proceed."

Mustafa Yurdabak

Republic of Turkey Prime Ministry Privatization Administration

"This book which reflects a young leader's perspective has brought a new point of view to management, administratorship and leadership by using a new generation, sincere, pure and faithful words."

Metin Akman

TUSIAD Board Member

"When I read the book's title 'Leadership Management Administatorship', the first idea came in my mind that how these three far-reaching and different issues are examined, interpreted and concluded in a single book. However, as I read the book written by a very young author, Aybars Öztuna, by means of my experience and practice, I have noticed that how proper, balanced and right the topic is discussed, interpreted and transmitted to the reader. Therefore, I sincerely congratulate and with a continued success to my friend, young author Aybars Öztuna who has put signature to such a good work."

Kayhan Ünal

TMO (Turkish Grain Board) Deputy Director General and Board Member

"As I turned the pages, I saw a work in which a 1000 piece puzzle takes shape, words and terms associate with management concept in a meaningful way. That the book which brings a new perspective to the management concepts by using a simple and sincere language with metaphors from everyday life have been written by a young writer at high school age is a great achievement. I believe that Aybars Öztuna will advance in authorship in the forthcoming years and become one of the leading figures of Turkey."

Kağan Kalınyazgan

TÖDER Vice President, Chairman of the Yüce Schools

"In his book, the author has shared "leadership" concept with suggestions and given the answer of the question "can leadership be learned or are you born with it" to us.

You, Aybars Öztuna, the world needs good-hearted, hard-working and visionary leaders like you."

Saadet Roach

EAQUALS Supervisor, Nesibe Aydın Schools General Manager

"Success is actually obtained by differentiating from general "success" criteria and creating a difference. Such a young writer has already created this difference. In this book he does not provide a prescription about being a good leader or manager. Rather, he intimately asks right questions. The main point is rather than giving ready answers asking right questions at the right time, isn't it?"

Serap Dedeoğlu

TMMOB (Union of Chambers of Turkish Engineers and Architects) İMO (Chamber of Civil Engineers) Deputy Secretary General

Foreword

Leaders, managers, management systems are concepts that affect our lives directly or indirectly. I present this work which synthesizes past, present and future in our daily lives, theory and practice to you, my valuable readers. In this work, I wish to address not only to leaders and managers, to people who want to shed light on their lives and strive to renew their perspectives in order to be an effective leader and manager.

Leadership and Life Management in Family

Family is the first and fundamental community that each individual faces for the first time in his life. In addition, it is the place where basic values and most part of the life have actualized. Individuals who have no family or have lost their family could also continue their life depending on their individual efforts and psychology. We cannot say that leaders have all grown up in a family environment, but family is among the main factors for the growth and development of individuals. We can say that particularly parents, parenting style, every situation at home and lots of things have direct impact on individual's and leader's life. In this context, revealing the leadership qualification or destroying this qualification originate from the family. Even though this qualification is supported or hindered, it depends largely on the individual. Therefore, if we define parents of leaders or people who train them as also role model, advisor or leader directly, it would not be wrong. In addition, at task sharing in family life, we face leadership again. Person who makes decisions in the

1

family is usually the leader of that family. If everyone in the family has something to say in the decision-making process, then there are several leaders in that family. However, if there is a guiding and prominent leader when all ideas have clashed, then things can be put in order in an easier way.

In fact, individuals who lead and serve as a model to each other are leaders. Together with this, parents are the basic entities that will lead to the child in the family. Their attitude is very important in the upbringing of the child as a leader. In that case, it would not be an exaggeration if we say that foundation of leadership of an individual is laid in the family.

Alternate Paths

Not only in leadership and management, do not assume that everything will go smoothly in all areas of your life, you will always be successful and have time. One day you would be wrong. Do not think that you will remember everything, no you cannot remember. Do not think you will solve every problem and setbacks, no you cannot solve. They are inevitable and facts of life.

Your plan may go as you wish or may not go too well. So, no matter what happens, do you have a second plan? If you do not have, you may face a crisis. Let's say you get through this crisis. Suppose that you have troubles again, do you have a third alternative?

In fact, it is not possible to find alternative ways at every issue in our lives. So, what should we do then?

We have to be prepared for the case that things go wrong.

If things go wrong, we have to set out to solve them without panic and despair.

We should not forget that at the end we can be either successful or fail. Instead of looking upon failure as negativity or disaster, we should make a sacrifice to take lesson.

If you pay attention to these three basic warnings, I believe that you will be much more relaxed, happy, and successful. However, when it comes to management and leadership, things can change a bit. An effective leader and manager does not set out without determining the second and third alternative routes, if he sets out then he may have become an effective leader who can surpass problems that he encounters by means of his experience.

I repeat again that leaders and managers are not alone; there is a team or group at the backstage. So he cannot act irresponsibly. He should not forget that responsibility of the business, life and team is on him and he should shape his steps accordingly.

Analytical and Holistic Thinking

Thinking is one of the most important things that we do in the intensive flow of our lives. Here our thoughts are important. At this point, knowing which thinking system that we have, how to create and develop our thinking system and then how to execute our thoughts are of paramount importance.

All individuals in the world are different and everyone's way of thinking is also special. In general, when we look at the issue scientifically, way of thinking is categorized into two groups called analytic thinking and holistic thinking:

Analytical Thinking

Is the way of thinking which is conducted to draw conclusion by decomposing information and considering the elements making up the result. In this thinking system, you will decompose information as if you are separating your team into units and then you will handle the scope.

Holistic Thinking

Is the thinking system which is carried out so as to conclude from the broad perspective. In this thinking system, without separating or being separated into units, you will handle the scope in the general sense.

Leadership in Knowledge Acquisition

How important is knowledge for you? What is the difference between ignorance and wisdom? Knowledge is the sum of the data within the scope of any subject. Every subject has a separate statement and philosophy. Some of them are similar but some are very different. Explanation and proving of these statements and philosophies take place with the knowledge. Today, numerous information sources and countless wise people are available. Qualifying knowledge, differentiating as knowledgeable or ignorant is completely wrong. Not everyone has to be knowledgeable and they do not have to be knowledgeable with the same subject. Therefore, everyone is different. Everyone's abilities, way of thinking, manner of application is different. That is why everything that exists is unique. Suppose that we have a hundred flowers of the same kind, but to some of these flowers we only give water, to the other ones we give nutrient water which will provide them to grow better. As you predict, flowers in these two groups will grow differently. Or if you train your dog it will do what you want, but if you let your dog out, it will be brought up differently. Let's continue with our examples. If you start teaching different languages to a child as of birth, a few years later, he will have command of many languages, but if you teach just one language to another child, he will only have a command of single language. Of course there may be exceptions, but in general it is like that. While you are constantly working to develop yourself and trying to gain information on many issues, someone else may not try to work to have knowledge or improve himself. Therefore, I respect everyone. Before starting to criticize a person, I think that I must have a lifestyle like him and have a way of thinking like him. This is not possible. Both knowledge and ignorance can be interpreted like this. However, having knowledge about many issues may be beneficial for you. Yes, it can provide I said. Just because having knowledge does not mean that you will apply them or you will not forget them for a lifetime. Therefore having knowledge will open the door of being effective leader-manager to you, on the other side applying and using the knowledge will make you an effective individual-leader.

Knowledge Management

Is knowledge something you think that you should own or possess? Knowledge is a concept reliability and accuracy of which is dealt within the current evaluation framework. Technology, internet and social media are very serious sources with regard to imposing incorrect information as the right information or vice versa.

Having more knowledge and being wise do not stand for being smart and efficient. As long as knowledge is used, developed and harmonized with life, it is useful and necessary. Raw information is just a waste of time. At both learning and implementation stages, knowledge management is necessary. Then what is knowledge management and how does it occur?

Knowledge management is a management system that covers the learning, synthesis and implementation phases of knowledge. In general, this management may express the position of people with knowledge but it may differ on people. Everyone has different learning, synthesis and application power, abilities and intelligence. Therefore knowledge management is subjective and different in terms of method. At this point, the control and distribution of information on common ground should be elaborated.

<u>Knowledge Control</u>

It is comparison and inspection of the knowledge that the individual and his surrounding have.

<u>Knowledge Distribution</u>

It is distribution of the scope and the subject of knowledge and ensuring the distributional transition. When knowledge is applied, it is very powerful. When there is knowledge, knowledge management is essential. Knowledge management varies between individuals. The principal of this variety is based on self-knowledge.

Individual Leadership-Administratorship-Management

As it is understood from the term individual, it is an individual oriented approach. Due to our subject, this statement will be covered in two chapters. One of them is individual-oriented approach, the other one focuses on understanding the other person which is on the opposite side of the individual. We will examine these contents in leadership, administratorship and management areas.

Individual Leadership

Individual leadership, can be handled in two scope as self-leadership of the individual and leadership of the individual to another individual.

• Self-Leadership of the Leader

It is realized by the leadership of the leader himself on self-government and sovereignty basis, which we'll discuss in detail in the following pages. First, leader starts with knowing himself and taking the lead of himself.

- Leadership of the Individual to another Individual

As we will discuss in the following pages, we will see this under the scope of Coaching in Leadership.

The goal here is the one person-centered leadership ability of the leader. Therefore, individual coaching can be an example to this.

As well as these, place can be given to individual leadership depending on the strategy of the leader under the framework of inductive approach namely reaching the target by using individual-oriented target.

- Self-Leadership of the Manager

Every manager does not have leadership characteristic. However, even standards in his daily life, may cause individual leadership. His order and attitudes during the management may also affect individual leadership directly or indirectly. The self-improvement in the topics that he is short or has a grasp even can be interpreted as a part of individual leadership.

- Leadership of the Manager to another Individual

Manager as the name implies, is the person who manages. He manages small or large communities. I would like to remind that, leadership of him to the people that he manages is beyond the scope of this topic. That issue is under scope of team leadership. The issue that we address is the understanding that is individual oriented, that is to say that has individual goals. Consequently, assuming that the manager is individual-oriented, leadership of the manager to another individual will be concerned. Anyway, team is made up of are individuals.

In this context, we can say that individual leadership in management takes place in both scopes.

• Leadership in Management Approach

When we consider the strategy and double-sided management approach, we can talk about individual leadership in management approach.

During the transition between management, individuals are at stake during the relationship between manager-team and manager-team-others. Also, marketing concept is built on individuals. In short, individual leadership in management becomes more of an issue.

Managing Diversity

Our life consists of diversity. When you look at your environment, you can observe that different concepts come together. We can use the term as variation. Here, we prefer diversity.

Every human being is a separate world, each world is a particular variety. That is why everyone is different. Some vary with physically, some intellectually and some with respect to skills. These are diversities. We can say that, people create an outline of the general diversity by means of their relationship with everything inside and around them.

Every individual has characteristics that he owns or feels that he owns. These two are different. Some accept themselves as is and some wants to show themselves different from the usual self. They can also bring about the diversity among themselves. Essentially environment, ambiance and people are entirely built on diversity. This diversity brings along cultural, ethnic, financial, spiritual, political, historical, geographical, religious reflections. There are people who recognize these reflections and regard them as different values and also there are people who disregard them and act with the understanding that states 'world is a whole'. Accuracy or fallacy of this is open to debate and comment is up to you. However, it is not possible to ignore the diversity around us. Indeed, people who act in defiance of this understanding can suffer a variety of issues, including communication.

In leaders and managers, individual diversity, team diversity, diversity internal and external to the organization, direct and indirect diversities are available. Leaders-managers who act in line with this understanding will become effective. Since managing multiple people yields diversity and differences evenly. This is one of the basic elements of communication between managements. Mastery and efficiency of Leaders who care in this direction will enhance. Generally, we confront with two types of understanding on this issue: an understanding and the one against it. In other words they are opposite to each other. In particular, this does not change. However, this is a violation of diversity and authenticity. Other understandings that are against these two understanding or accepting them constitute diversity. As well as those, a person can be environmental-friendly, author, musician and leader. Here it reveals the characteristics and differences in people again. Then, diversity may also occur.

Diversity in the understanding of management is essential. Just like in our lives. We ought to control it well, appreciate all kinds of varieties regardfully and take advantage of this diversity. For example in relation to the culture, sending an Asian person to the negotiations in

Asia will enable a quicker result. As I will mention in the communication section, every culture has its own characteristics and these can gain an opposite meaning for other cultures. In order to eliminate it acting within frame of that culture or assigning someone who knows that culture will be useful. You may not have people who know the culture of the work you have done. At this point it is necessary to examine and recognize that culture and act accordingly.

Being Focused on Solutions

If we divide missions, visions, aims and expectations of the people into three categories, they will be being start-access focused; being process-development focused and being result-solution focused.

<u>Being start-access focused:</u> It is based on the idea that aims to get into any event or circumstance. This idea argues that things will get back on the rails as you go along.

For example: "When I get into a good college, the rest will follow it."

<u>Being process-development focused:</u> It is based on the idea that attaches importance to the development, process and gain in any event or circumstance.

<u>Being result-solution focused:</u> It is based on the idea that focuses on the solution and obtaining result after having problems in any event or circumstance. Rather than planting and growing a tree, it focuses on getting fruit from that tree.

This is the essence of these three basic categories. These three approaches are the necessities of leadership.

Essentially, three orientations complement each other. Well, which way of thinking is within the scope of effective leadership? All of them. However, purpose and scope may vary from person to person. Each responsibility is a different perspective and a different world.

At each work and responsibility, different requirements are priorities. In this context, when you adapt these three way of thinking to the current situation and condition you will demonstrate effective leadership qualities.

Consultant

Consultant is the person to whom people consult about any subject or scope. Consult concept appears as counseling and advisement. Consultancy is actually a profession. It is a serious and important task. Today, the main factor that is active on the effective leader is consultants. Especially for young leaders, importance of this matter should be comprehended. I have many on-going studies about this issue.

Consultants not only serve the leader. They can operate in all areas including sports and music but they should have a full command in the area they operate and they should communicate well.

Do not forget that effective leaders have effective consultants and effective consultants have effective ideas ...

Managing Change

Leadership and administratorship are dynamic. They renew themselves continuously and they are ready for the change and take advantage of it. Everything around us has been changing. These changes will impact on our lives either positively or negatively. In particular, definition, recognition and application stages of the change are important in administratorship. In fact, leaders and managers who do not pay attention to the change will suffer from the change.

Let's examine the change by separating it into two categories:

External Factors

Internal Targets

External Factors: Change comes from outside and ready for use. Results brought by the development of the technology can be an example to this. Offers, activities and practices of another company are another example. Controlling external factors is more difficult.So, at any moment and anywhere, they can be faced with. In order to overcome this, being open to change and innovation and having a well-equipped team in every sense are necessary.

Internal Targets: Change of company, institution and requirements are preferable. To ensure the dynamism, targets and preferences can be determined. In this context, as a result of targets consisting of internal factors, change can be applied in every field. Change of contacts, change of activities, change of projects, change of strategy and change of materials can be

examples to them. If we examine these examples:

- Change of People: When you cannot get yield or when you want more yield, you can change people. This change can be between companies or tasks. In accordance with the content, development of people can also be mentioned. Personal development is also a change. At this point, additional training will be helpful to offer further development opportunities for people. These can be provided by the company as well as people can provide them by their opportunities.

- Change of Activities: In order to improve all activities, get better results and attain targets which have different foundations, this method can be applied.

- Change of Projects: Projects may be inadequate, deficient and inefficient. At this point, change is needed. Change of projects expresses this.

- Change of Strategy: Strategies do not always remain constant.

- There is no requirement to go always in the same direction. Therefore, according to target and requirement, change of specific aspects or the whole of strategies is important at this point.

- Change of Materials: From the goods to the interview environment, all settings, goods and materials may need to be changed. Change can be applied to get profit or make the environment effective.

So, what are the changes in your mind? To what extent these changes affect you? Today's world is constantly changing and change is inevitable. Therefore, being ready for it in every area of your life will enable you to get more comfortable way. Hoping that the changes change you and you change the changes ...

Assuring Balance

Assuring balance emerges in many points about the principles of leadership and administratorship. Assuring balance which has an important place in the management philosophy is also called as balance policy and is an extremely important requirement.

Balance is assured between many areas including people-parties-issues-systems-principles and must be assured as well. Leaders who are able to establish balance will be located in the upper levels of leadership. Balance does not mean equality or being at an equal distance to everyone. It means giving necessary weight to the necessary side. Showing more importance to the side that needs care most, and showing less importance to the other side is also an example of balance. This feature is the confusing characteristic of the balance. It should be well known and distinguished.

Dynamism

Dynamism is known as vitality. Ensuring dynamism is an indication of vitality and activity. More particularly this concept is important in leadership. In fact more place should be given to this concept in our lives and it should be internalized. Let's exemplify the word dynamism with a statement that I frequently use in politics. "The importance of young people should not be forgotten in ensuring the dynamism in politics." This example is also applicable to leadership and administratorship scopes. Dynamism may appear in many areas and scopes. Strengthening the dynamism and emphasizing it, will put forward innovation, expansion of perception and different ideas.

Disciplinary

According to its word meaning, disciplinary has two meanings. First one is science, second one is strict order. An example of science is chemistry discipline, example to strict order is leader discipline.

As of our subject, we will focus on order and discipline. Discipline is one of the basic concepts used in leadership, administratorship and in particular management field. If discipline is not effectively and balanced used, it is difficult to handle. Today, when the subject is discipline, strict policies come to our mind. Whereas, discipline makes sense to the extent it is applied. Indeed, very strict policies digress from effective characteristic. Discipline is not only confined to individuals . It is divided into four sub disciplines as self-discipline, interpersonal discipline, team discipline and group discipline.

Self-Discipline: It is individual's own discipline. It includes commitment to own order. A person who cannot control his own discipline, will have difficulties to control other disciplines.

Interpersonal Discipline: Is the discipline between the people. It takes place between the person/people who apply and maintain discipline.

Team Discipline: It is important especially in management mentality and refers to the discipline of entire team.

Group Discipline: Is the discipline owned by any group. The best example of it is military discipline.

We can basically cover disciplines like that. More statements will be included in the details. The subject is really important,because internalization and application of disciplines have importance. Without discipline, many things will suffer. Consequently, it is needed to grasp and apply discipline at necessary degree. For the sake of examining these degrees:

1. Passive Discipline: Passive discipline consists of the application of discipline at weakest level. It refers to the discipline at minimum degree.

2. Controlled Discipline: It is the controllable discipline. It is more effective than passive discipline. Corruption in passive discipline does not occur in controlled discipline.

3. Active Discipline: It is the active discipline understanding and there is a continuing pattern.

4. Dominant Discipline: Is the full application of discipline and refers to the rule of order.

5. Solid Discipline: Is the discipline applied by many leaders by mistake and it usually results in negative and less efficient consequences or failure. It means

the strict discipline and not compromising it under any circumstances.

Which discipline would you prefer? How their consequences will affect you and other person/people to whom you have applied discipline? Apply them soon and see the results. Accordingly, with the experience that you have gained, take a firm stand and attain success. This is because discipline is not limited by theory. Things you have read will show you the path and implementing them will lead you to walk on that path.

Intellectual Leadership / Management / Administratorship

Steps you take consist of your thoughts. Therefore, your thoughts will always be in the forefront of your life. Which form of intellectuality do you think you are in? Can you dominate your thoughts? So, how do you shape your thoughts? While we have been thinking about the answers of these questions, let's go back to the management again.

Management philosophy was formed with ideas. In fact, all of those philosophies were formed with ideas. For example; formation of painting, music and dance is rooted in the idea to express oneself, tell something and communicate the idea. Additionally,when the issue is our feelings, we cannot decide logically. But our feelings are also thoughts. Everything in our life is made up of thoughts. Some are communicated; some are implemented; and some remain as only thought, expression and icon.

Effective thinking is possible by making thoughts effective. It can be possible by constantly thinking, ripening, upbringing and developing thoughts. Therefore, especially for leaders and managers, effective thinking approach is extremely important and it will direct influence over the decisions taken and the work with the team.

As well as these, now we do not encounter so much, but I guess, there is a system that will be actualized in the future. This is the intellectual leadership. According to this system, intellectual leaders will lead the way to the managers in the company about the decisions to take and not to take. By this way, actual managing entity will be intellectual leaders and managers will be at implementing side.

As a different expressions of the same system, people who have leader appearance or at leader position will be able to professionalize in the light of intellectual leader's experience and knowledge. For example, intellectual leaders who are at their homes can lead managers about what to do before meeting via telephone or different forms of communication. As a result, spiritual leaders will emerge who undertake brain function.

Today, there are company or manager consultants. They are partial intellectual leaders. Different from the issue that I mentioned above, consultant may not have leadership knowledge. Having knowledge about the issue may be accepted as sufficient. Alternatively, the intellectual leaders are the ones who specialized in leadership, management and administration in person and have the brain function.

Depressors

One of the inevitable issues in our lives is depressors. Depressors are the ones who are trying to lower our success, motivation and any positive activity. I always use the same expression for depressors. "When they try to depress us, they actually disgrace themselves." Depressors are unskilled, non-wise, pseudo-intellectual people who were at the bottom stage of the leadership ladder. At this point obviously, wise people and senior managers may also have depressing feature due to ambition. This does not change the fact that unskilled, non-wise, pseudo-intellectual people are at the bottom of the leadership ladder.

However, successful or real leaders may show depressing qualities if they succumb to greed. No matter they show leadership qualities, when they show depressing attitudes, subsequently they lost their leadership qualities.

Then we can ask few questions. How to deal with depressors? How to handle depressors so as to be affected from them at least level?

Depressors are inevitable. It is impossible to completely get rid of them. They can be nearby or distant. The best way to deal with the depressors is to maintain your own line. Continue on your way, without abandoning your own principles, goals and objectives. As well, there is no point I being obstinate, stubbornly insisting on discussing things with these people. Walking away and ignoring them is of great importance. They are just jealous, hung-up individuals who have no expectations for their own lives.

Team Leadership

Team leadership is a concept that we frequently encounter in management and administratorship areas. A community made up of at least two people for any purpose is called team. Today, we know that single-person centered management loses its validity. At this point we can say that an effective team will be superior to an effective leader. This is a serious comparison and affects management systems to a large extent. The team leader is the pioneer team member for any team. It is likely to have several team leaders in teams but having only one leader who comes forward and becomes prominent is more probable and necessary.

So, on which basis an effective team should be based and how should this be?

Interpersonal Relations, Communication, Compliance: 40%

Individual Behaviors, Characteristics: 35%

Knowledge about Subject: 15%

Experience: 10%

Another important question is with whom and for which purpose the team is created. Foundations of the team know the purpose, establishing appropriate configuration according to that purpose, selecting suitable people and providing necessary harmonization among the people.

Let's examine types of teams, based on their aims:

<u>Topic Based Team:</u> It is established about or around a topic. It can be described as an expert team.

<u>Result Based Team:</u> It is a result-focused partnership and way of working. Instead of external factors, getting result as soon as possible is important.

<u>Requirement Based Team:</u> Team is created due to a financial or moral requirement which is either voluntarily or involuntarily.

<u>Effective Team:</u> It is a fixer team which can cope with every topic and span and also compatible with each other regardless of any interest.

As the team is based on an aim, achievements and results are indispensable for the team. A community which is formed without any purpose that does not attain any achievement or result is not a team. It does not demonstrate team feature and only limited to community. In this context, it is an absolute necessity that the team engage in activities such as self-measurement, evaluation and orientation. These measurement, evaluation and orientation can take place in many areas. If we discuss the scope of these areas:

<u>Team Related Measurement, Assessment and Orientation:</u> It is the team's self-measurement, assessment and orientation. The main criterion is the individual himself.

Team Related Measurement, Assessment and Orientation: It is the team's self-measurement, assessment and orientation. Basic criteria are individuals and teams.

Gain Related Measurement, Assessment and Orientation: It is the measurement, assessment and orientation of gains. Basic criterion is the gains.

Processual Measurement, Assessment and Orientation: It is the measurement, assessment and orientation of the process. Basic criteria are the process and things done or being done.

Result Related Measurement, Assessment and Orientation: It is the measurement, assessment and orientation of the result. The result is the basic criteria.

Situational Measurement, Assessment and Orientation: It is the measurement, assessment and orientation of the situation. The main criterion is the situation.

Measurement, Assessment and Orientation of the Team Leader: It is the measurement, assessment and orientation of the team leader. The main criterion is the leader.

Measurement, Assessment and Orientation by the Team Leader: Is the measurement, assessment and orientation conducted by the team leader. Basic criterion is the team.

Critical Leadership

Can you tolerate criticism? Can you do self-criticism? Can you criticize someone else or others?

Criticism is a very important concept to brainstorm ideas in a multi-idea scheme. Criticism requires idea, knowledge accumulation and experience. Of course, every criticism is not necessarily reasonable or right. Actually there is no correctness or fallacy for a criticism. Criticism is subjective, so anything that you criticize may be blue for you and according to other people it may be green. At this point, criticism reinforces the connection between thoughts and ideas and also is associated with developmental leadership in a supportive way.

Criticism seems like a negative concept which is done only negatively, but essentially it can be done both in a positive and negative sense.

Critical leadership is a concept which is the synthesis of criticism and leadership. We will cover the scope of this concept in three categories:

Criticizing Yourself: Self-criticism is not a characteristic that everyone can do. Most people usually do not want to see their bad and negative aspects, some of them think that they are flawless and others cannot notice their mistakes or assume that they notice these mistakes. On the other hand, some cannot see their positive aspects. In this context, the self-criticism ability is very important. Whenever necessary, we should see the full side of the cup, and whenever necessary we should see the empty side of it. Synthesis and application of both generate effective self-criticism.

Criticizing Others: it is a concept that refers to criticize others. Making Comparison between Criticisms: It is the comparison of criticizing yourself, criticizing others and other criticisms around you. It can be applied by the steps collecting,merging, synthesizing, comparing criticisms respectively.

Critical leadership does not have any additional activity different from this description. However leadership is the source of criticism and has the essential importance in critical leadership. It involves criticism of the leadership qualities, criticizing the leaders and the criticism made by the leader.

Effective Leadership

Effective understanding is a concept that is very valuable to reach certain conclusions in all areas. Being active in any subject or field will bring along domination to that subject or field, success and correct choices.

The effective leader is the ideal leader. Yet, leadership cannot be ideal, ethical and best without being effective. Therefore, effective leadership is the highest point of leadership, namely its summit. Therefore, it is extraordinarily difficult to reach this summit. Until now, highest levels of the leadership have been defined as the best leader, the ideal leader, the ethical leader and so on. However, these definitions are increasingly inadequate now and I think they will lose their effect in the following years. I also have noted the important points that will take you to effective leadership in this book. Everyone is a leader at a certain level, but very few people are effective leaders. In other words, let's take the word activity which is done by students after lesson. The root of the word activity is active. Well, then we can define the activity as the action to learn the topic in an active way. In this respect if we express good leaders as lesson, we can express effective leaders as lesson plus activity.

If we simplify good leadership and effective leadership concepts, it will be enough to say that good is a relative concept. Furthermore, the effective leadership concept may be considered as relatively good. If particular concepts are added to effective leadership, it will no longer be relative. To sum up, effective leadership concept differs from the good leadership with respect to the principles it has.

Effective leadership does not only mean that leadership is effective. Effective leadership is a principle, an ideal, a level itself. This level is the highest level of leadership. Therefore, leaders can be effective, provided that they have implemented all of the requirements needed to achieve this level.

Leadership process is like a never-ending marathon. Even you participate in the marathon at an early age and gain success, actual success is continuing this throughout your life. Reaching to the highest level of leadership means being an effective leader, but it does not mean that you have completed everything, you have performed well but you have a lot of work to do. Therefore, effective leadership is the last and most difficult level of leadership and if you attain this level, do not get the wrong idea about staying there forever. If you do not improve yourself and do not maintain your effectiveness, you will go down the stairs one by one that you have climbed before. Leadership is easy and also difficult at the same time isn't it?

Developmental Leadership /
Management / Administratorship

I know a few people who have dedicated their life to self-development and these people adopt their continuous improvement, making better and learning more as a principle. Some of them has graduated from two or three universities and have been continuing their profession and others just read book so as to move in this direction. Some of them works interdisciplinary (e.g. in sports, music and technology fields) and some develop themselves in a fixed field (for example, by conducting administratorship in different companies).

Everyone does not have developmental behavior and activity logic. On the contrary, there are people who have only one profession and work at the same position for their lifetime. The same issue is valid for leaders and managers. While some managers are active in many different companies and fields, others do not get out of their company or field.

Developmental leadership is actually about the way of thinking. It depends on your life, your expectations, your goals, your objectives and activities. The basic point in management is to manage and have the principles which are developed in this frame. If you show a developmental performance, you can work in many areas of management and you will be successful. By means of developmental way of thinking, you will be open to an unending development throughout your life, hence you will build your life plan accordingly.

For leaders and managers being developmental influences not only the leader person, but also his team and environment. At this direction, leaders may shed light to their environment and team and these leaders can provide them to discover themselves.

Assignment

Being able to do everything is no longer valid for leaders. Within the frame of current and future leadership understanding, this concept is certainly insufficient.

Effective leader is the person who can lead and manage every level and scope. However here managing everything does not stand for omniscience and doing everything. It means managing in the most effective manner by means of assignments in a supportive way. In fact, this property is located on the upper levels of leadership and management ladder.

For issues at which effective leader does not have comprehensive knowledge, he can assign the task to the individual who has a grasp of that issue. Similarly when he has comprehensive knowledge about an issue, he can also assign the task to others in order to create different perspectives about that issue. After the task assignment, following the assigned person, decision making and reaching to a conclusion are under the responsibility of leaders.

Visual Angle

Perspective, visual angle, perception, holistic perspective and analytical perspective are maybe separate concepts but they can be gathered under the same roof. This roof can be referred as observation. All of the concepts under this roof are the primary deterministic qualifications in leadership and management,since every committed activity and adopted order take place on the basis of this perspective. If we examine these concepts:

> Perspective: Refers to the side and the angle that the observation takes place.

> Visual Angle: Refers to the noticed portion of the observation.

> Perception: Implies that the observation has been understood and perceived.

Holistic Perspective: Refers to looking from a distance, a broader perspective and seeing the whole.

Analytical Perspective: Refers to looking from closer, a narrower perspective separately and seeing by means of decomposition.

So, among these perspectives, which one of them is within the scope of effective leadership or which perspectives belong to a higher level manager? Effective leader: Is the one who has all of these perspectives, examines the events with different observations, evaluates, synthesizes and implements necessary actions.

Leadership in Our Daily Lives

In our daily life we are leading many topics, consciously or unconsciously. We may notice many of them and at the same time we may not notice many of them. Identifying the things to do, programming them, arranging their time schedule, organizing them according to their variation, implementing this organization, comparing the effects as a result of the implementation are part of the leadership in our daily lives.

Leadership is not confined to a single qualification, if it is, then that qualification is not leadership. From market to cinema, theater to work, library to town, laboratory to parliament, in every environment and at every action of us we are under the influence of leadership.

Every individual, regardless of different areas and standards, is a leader. This cycle further increases the efficiency and individual leadership brings about social leadership and unity. Eventually an environment emanates which develops and renews itself each passing day. Maintaining high motivation in daily life is not a permanent situation. Therefore, doing like that will play a major role to enable efficiency to increase. If an individual pioneers a person about an issue at least once during his life, it reveals that, the individual is a leader. Being leader of your own before anyone else, self-criticism, managing and developing yourself are the essential characteristics that should be included in our daily lives and leaders. Firm steps always reveal themselves in a positive way.

We must take control of our lives literally, we should reveal the leadership in our lives more and we should be in struggle for developing ourselves in different areas. When we think about our lives, we should be individuals who notice that we have been taking the lead at various levels, endogeny and relate to our daily lives, make an effort to question and develop ourselves in this direction, serve as an example to the people and follow in other's good examples.

Culture in Our Daily Lives

Culture is a unique feature of a community but it is not limited to this. Culture is available in certain areas. For example; sports culture, music culture and so on. In this context, it is not wrong to express that culture is the characteristics pertain to the issue that the culture is associated with. Culture is at everywhere. Language which is important in communication is one of the features of the culture. Being cultured will improve your point of view, approaches to events and knowledge. This will contribute to you and your decisions.

We have talked about culture in management understanding and cross-cultural diversity in the Managing Diversity section. We will continue over the cultural leadership. Essentially, cultural leadership is not a different kind of leadership. Leaders who are cultured have been called cultural leader. It is not one of the basic requirements of the leadership but it is not an issue that can be omitted. Culture develops thoughts, thoughts affect decisions and finally decisions bring along management skills and leadership. Every leader cannot be a cultural leader. As every leader cannot be effective, every cultural leader cannot be effective as well. However, cultural leadership is a part of effective leadership.

Culture plays an important role not only in the government but also in our lives. There is no limit for culture, it is a concept that constantly evolves and needs improvement. This concept is like this for people. Examining cultural differences and having interdisciplinary knowledge will develop individual's perspective and brings with personal development and developmental leadership as well.

Trust, Trustworthiness

Is trust an abstract or concrete concept? Is this concept which we frequently encounter an important concept for you? Is the principle of trust among the key elements in the formation of your personality and characteristics?

In communication and even communication without words, more generally in interpersonal sentiment and stability mechanism, trust will play an extremely important role. Due to distrust, preference change, company selection, change of friend and environmental have been at stake and will continue to be like that. In leadership and management understandings, mutual trust is important for both parties. In cases where there is no trust or deficiency of trust, there are problems or will be in the future. In any order, trust is the basic choice. Of course, we cannot say that in every success, there also exists trust. We have encountered situations in which success is obtained without trust and we will continue to encounter them. Surely, while evaluating these, there must be a difference, a deficiency or excessiveness or an exceptional situation and this should not be overlooked. It should be noted that trust is essential and important. For this reason, leaders are the trustworthy ones.

Today and in the history, emergence of untrustworthy people as leaders aims to change the perception of leadership. In particular, mutual trust, individual confidence and self-confidence are the basic concepts in this scope.

<u>Mutual Trust:</u> Is formed by exhibiting the sense of trust in a bilateral way.

<u>Individual Trust:</u> Is one-sided version of mutual trust. Here the trust occurs by demonstrating it in a unilateral way.

<u>Self-Confidence:</u> Trust of oneself to his own.

To sum up, trust plays an important role in leadership and management. Principle of trustworthiness is included among the requirements of the effective leadership. Mutual trust and individual trust refer to this point. In addition to these, self-confidence which is the trust that the person feels about himself is a part of effective leadership. Since self-confidence reveals itself at people who know and dominate themselves, but of course excessive self-confidence limited itself to self-righteousness.

Dominance

Dominance is the mastery of any subject and having understanding about that subject in any way. Dominance is established by means of entirely grasping a subject or a work. Dominance in leadership and management is an essential issue, manager's dominance in the decisions taken, issues mentioned and instructions given speeds up the business and at the same time, missing dominance due to the leader and manager may slows down the business and create a negative impact.

Dominance in leadership and management is made up of several steps; Weak dominance, settled dominance, basic dominance, strong dominance and full dominance. If we look at these steps:

Weak dominance: Dominance which is below the basic dominance It is almost like a thin rope. It can break off at any moment.

Settled dominance: An understanding of dominance foundation of which has been established. It has settled.

Basic Dominance: An understanding of dominance, foundation of which is firm and unshakable.

Strong Dominance: This is an understanding that does not compromise its dominance and an absolute dominance is at stake.

Full Dominance: Even small concessions are rejected and dominance has been applied within the frame of the principles.

When leaders and managers have dominance and full understanding over the business and obtain all kinds of knowledge and experience, efficiency and distance travelled will increase at the same rate.

Dominance can also be determined by body language. Body languages of leaders and managers actually express whether they have established their dominance in that area. Leader who has a good command of a subject will express this by means of his attitudes and behaviors.

Addressing people, communicating effectively with people, being speechmaker, choosing the right data to convince people ... They play a significant role in leadership and management. In fact, people who fail on persuasion and communication are not expected to be a leader or manager. Just because, people who have difficulty in establishing communication are not found to be adequate to climb the managerial ladder.

You can be a leader or a manager by not talking or just talking ... Indeed, communication is not limited to words. It is possible to communicate by means of body language or many different ways. The basic principle in the relationship between leader and manager is the area between the parties. If leader and manager make themselves to be understood, get their way and activate them, they can climb the ladder. As well as these, simply communication is not enough. Convincing other people, applying this ability and specializing on it will develop you, your administration, and your leadership and also they will show your progress towards effective leadership.

You can use many ways to persuade people. Let's look at some of the elements that you should pay attention while you are persuading:

- Dominance in yourself and your explanation
- Dominance in topic
- Being honest and trustworthy
- Being lean, transparent and understandable
- Recognizing others, building empathy
- Preparing common ground
- Giving place to supportive qualifications
- Offering examples, statistics and graphical evidences
- Being authentic

Harmonic Management

The word harmony is among borrowed words. It also means congruence and consonance. Also we face the term harmony in music. It is used to qualify the conformity of sounds in music. We encounter this term at concordance of notes, multi-instrumental music and polyphonic music. Therefore, orchestra management is also corresponds to harmonic management. Harmonic management refers to the compliance of leader or manager with himself, his team and his environment in terms of managerial skills and assessment. At this point, harmonic management brings along adaptation to surrounding, environment and people. This is a matter of importance for the leadership. Individuals who are not in harmony with themselves and their environment have become alienated and have difficulties to fulfill the principles and requirements of the leadership.

Mistakes

Which of us did not make mistakes or did everything correctly? Mistakes and remorse are irremediable things but they affect past, present and the future. We are not perfect, faultless and flawless. We choose our preferences by ourselves. Therefore, during our lives it is impossible not to make mistake and be flawless. In this regard, how do we evaluate our mistakes and move towards advantages from disadvantage by being minimally affected from these mistakes?

Mistakes do not affect us at one time only. They are carried from past to present, present to future and have influence over this time frame. The less we are affected from our mistakes and the less we make mistakes, the more we save time. So, how will we do that?

Particularly, I have been mentioning an issue about leadership. It is self-knowledge. If you know yourself and be aware of your right doings and wrong doings, there will be serious changes in your life. Some of those changes are minimizing the loss of time and taking lessons from the previous mistakes and remorse which are minimized now.

Leadership in Animals

Animals also are trying to perform their vital activities in the frame of their lives, just like people. When we look at more generally, the main and common objective of all living things is to stay alive. They work in order to survive and they organize their vital activities accordingly.

In animals we come across leadership in many instances. For example, leaders who direct flocks of birds, ducklings who follow and imitate their mothers, and shepherd's dog who heads sheep herd are the examples come to mind. Consequently explaining the leadership as term and approaching the subject only theoretically would be incomplete and inadequate. Therefore, I find any information, book or research about the leadership insufficient. Again, leadership is a qualification. So as to develop and differentiate this qualification, researches can be conducted. We have observed that there is leadership among animals. So, do you think that animals could be leaders in their world? If we take the matter a step further and ask the question: "Can animals be leaders not only in their own world, but also in our world?" Of course I do not mean that animals will manage us, have you ever encounter a dog which carries garbage that we litter or a cat which tries to revive its deceased friend by doing cardiac massage with its paws ... Or a loyal dog to its owner... I do not know if you think about it, our relations are losing importance with each passing day, we are not as loyal as a dog ... So, do they set example to us? Do they lead us and have a small or big touch in many areas of our lives? The decision is yours ...

Persuasive Skill

Addressing people, communicating effectively with people, being speechmaker, choosing the right data to convince people ... They play a significant role in leadership and management. In fact, people who fail on persuasion and communication are not expected to be a leader or manager. Therefore, people who have difficulty in establishing communication are not found to be adequate to climb the managerial ladder.

You can be a leader or a manager by not talking or just talking ... In fact, communication is not limited to words. It is possible to communicate by means of body language or many different ways. The basic principle in the relationship between leader and manager is the area between the parties. If leader and manager make themselves understood, get their way and activate them, they can climb the ladder. As well as these, simply communication is not enough. Convincing other people, applying this ability and specializing on it will develop you, your administratorship, and your leadership and also they will show your progress towards effective leadership.

You can use many ways to persuade people. Let's look at some of the elements that you should pay attention while you are persuading:

- Dominance in yourself and your explanandum
- Dominance in topic
- Being honest and trustworthy
- Being lean, transparent and understandable
- Recognizing others, building empathy
- Preparing common ground
- Giving place to supportive qualifications
- Offering examples, statistics and graphical evidences
- Being authentic

Dominance in yourself and your explanation: You should have an understanding that develops and specializes yourself, your communication and explanation skills. You should have dominance in yourself and your explanation.

Dominance in topic: Whatever your communication topic is, you should have dominance in your topic. Furthermore, you should prepare the necessary infrastructure and be able to answer any questions.

Being honest and trustworthy: You should be honest and trustworthy. You should not compromise on intimacy. Moreover, other people should not think that you are lying or you are immersing pressure to persuade him.

Being lean, transparent and understandable: You must be lean, you should avoid unnecessary expressions and detailed information. You should be transparent and comprehensible. What you say should not create conflict with what you consider. The language that you use must be understood by other people.

<u>Recognizing others, building empathy</u>: You should recognize others, you should pay attention to their body language and what they say during the conversation. You should be informed of (if you have the opportunity to) others. You should show empathy towards others, if you are able to think like others, you can easily recognize their perspective and use them in your phraseology.

<u>Preparing common ground</u>: You must discover common denominator of you and others. By means of preparing a common ground, you will find an easier and more effective way to agree and persuade.

<u>Giving place to supportive qualifications:</u> You must find supportive qualifications in your topic and narration. You can bring in this qualification by using metaphors, telling stories and adding wise sayings.

<u>Offering examples, statistics and graphical evidences:</u> Everyone's learning skills, ways of learning are different. Some use visual, some auditory, some physical, some rhythmic, some textual methods to learn. Also some uses more than one ... Therefore, when you include a little bit of all of them, this will carve you in stone. Giving examples and providing visual data statistically and graphically are more understandable for others. In addition, in some people right side of brain is dominant, while in some of them left side. This will have an effect on the individual's inclinations. While Left brain dominant people are inclined to analytical thinking, right brain dominant

people are inclined to art. (If you examine this issue in more detail, you may obtain interesting information.) Therefore, you should shape and develop your expression power according to each case.

<u>Being authentic:</u> I think this is the key point. You must be different from the others. If we go back to the beginning, you should discover yourself and reveal your authentic soul. Ultimately, you should also shape your narration. Consequently, since you are authentic, you will be different, since you are different, you'll be permanent.

After a little reminder, I'll leave the synthesis of this topic to you. This reminder is not just for the principles of persuasion, it is applicable in your life. Do not be cocky, if you are wise you won't be anyway, be humble, but don't overdo it.If you try too hard to convince them that you are not great or special,they might believe you.

Foresight

Foresight means declaring the future events, thinking about them and making estimation about them. This foresight may be for near or distant future. In fact, when we handle this opinion within the scope of thoughts, thoughts can be expressed in terms of estimates. Consistency of these thoughts depends on the analysis, synthesis and foresight abilities of the individual.

Some people ensure this qualification with sentiment, some with logic and thinking system and others with analysis-synthesis judgment.

Leaders who are located on the top leadership leader are foresighted and especially effective leaders. The most important reason for effective leaders to have this qualification is evaluating and synthesizing today by examining the past, exercising commentary and analysis power in the direction of objectives and scope for the future. Consistency of this view is already due to the scope of this definition.

Foresight is not only an opinion or a long-term estimate for the distant future. It involves every step in the future. Either a second later or million years later … In this context, effective leaders are planned, programmed ones who consider a few steps beyond and so they gain farsightedness.

Foresight is a serious business, its impact strength is very important. It is the first and most important consideration to help you to carve out your roadmap so as to realize your goals, plans, wishes and expectations.

Foresight is not a skill. It is actually a developable predictive power. Working to gain this vision or if you have it working again to improve it will be an important step towards your life and your decision. How about starting right now?

Communication in Leadership and Administration

Communication is a need between people in a continuous manner throughout life. In cases where the communication is not applied or imperfectly applied, mistakes and errors may occur.

In order to provide effective communication, individual must have strong communication with his own, have dominance over language that will be used in communication, establish reciprocal tolerance, respect and empathize during communication.

Effective leader implements the communication in a best and most efficient way. One of the common denominators of leadership and administratorship understandings is communication. Using communication badly, not attaching necessary importance and respect to communication will result in short-dated and foundationless steps.

Communication is very important for each individual in our daily life. It also comes evenly to the forefront in leadership and administratorship. Consequently, another feature that distinguishes effective leader from other leaders is communication.

Unlike other individuals, in leadership and administratorship, there must be constant communication efficiency. If the leader and manager experiences difficulties in the communication and the decisions and steps taken, time losses, negative results, and mistakes will arise in the work or objective. Therefore, leaders and managers must pursue a very careful, effective and efficient policy about communication.

Factors such as impression of leader on others during communication, direction, orientation, stimulation are also supportive for persuasive skill. In addition to these, selected words during communication, way of asking question may enable to get desired response from other or may end in undesired responses. In this sense, careful choice of words plays an important role in the practice of communication.

Communication is not limited to words and questions, of course. Equally, body language is a major component of communication.

The essence of communication in leadership and administration is the application of communication effectively in every sense.

First Impression

In our relationships, we try to have an idea about someone whom we see for the first time. We question what he is like, why he speaks or dresses like that. Apart from these, even for someone that we know, we can estimate how he takes care of an issue, whether he takes it seriously or heeds by the help of his impression on you. Consequently, first impression has importance for all of us.

I always say that first impression accounts for the half of overall impression. Of course, you can come across different instances. However in general, the first position and the first impression are very important. This is a kind of symbol, a form of expression. Therefore, we do not buy anything that does not please the eye or we do not like. This acceptance does not restricted to above and applies to interpersonal communication. If we talk about leadership and administratorship, a leader who starts his speech with the word "I", may cause others to feel insignificant.

Let's get some more details and see the functions of body language in the first impression:

Greetings: Although it changes according to traditions, in the common ground everyone greet, handshake or symbolizes it in a different way at the first time. This is also an indication of the interpersonal prestige. Even during handshaking, we see that message is conveyed in different ways. For example, if two hands are facing one another, it means equity between the parties whereas, when one palm looks to the ground during handshaking, that means, "I am superior than you" or "We are not equal". Of course, this kind of examples can be labelled as the interpretation of the expression of body language. Everyone does not execute their greeting by being aware of these.

Arrangement / Layout: The way you dressed, your style, cleaning of your clothes, personal hygiene, your smell, symbols you use or wear (if any), in short your appearance is among the main elements of the first impression.

Your Explanandum: Your posture, your expression, your body language, your speech, your own unique personality and characteristic can be easily observed in the first impression.

When we turn back to the first impression at leaders and managers, posture, movements, style of the leaders pose importance now and in the future. Asserting the contrary brings an understanding that remains the leadership so-called. The fundamental part of the overall impression is the first impression. This idea may vary among people, but the unchangeable principle is that the first impression will always have importance.

What do you think about first impression? How do you evaluate yourself about this topic? How should the other person have an impression, what do you think about this? At what extent this issue constitutes importance for leaders and managers?

Human Management

Human beings can be managed and manipulated just like other creatures. Each one is a unique and separate world which contains spiritual and logical variety in itself. I have used the term unique in order to explain its different qualification and the term separate world in order to explain different perspectives.

While managing people is not an easy task and process for people who are at the lower steps of leadership, it is actually an easy task for effective leaders. This management can be learned but this qualification cannot be found in individuals who do not involve in activities which will bring and consolidate leadership qualities and leadership itself. The basis of the difficulty to manage people is uniqueness of the people. People who have solved, embodied and also put into practice this issue is called an expert on human kind. People who recognize people well and also provide inter-managerial transition can also perform human management. Of course, being an expert on human kind is only half of human management. By applying this, having managerial equipment and leadership power, human management comes true.

We face with people and management in every area of our lives. Therefore, human management takes place at the most important and upper part of the leadership power and management systems and it is of paramount importance. Most of the effective leaders are capable of performing this, but few are not able to do it. Anyhow, it is not possible to realize it completely. Centre is human who is a living thing, not a machine. In particular, as people have intellectual and intuitive skills and variations, it is clear that performing this is difficult and it is impossible to perform this flawlessly.

Initiative

In the most critical moments of your life, at times which you regard as important or unimportant ,you may need to take the initiative. Initiative, responsibility and decision are choices. You need to perform these choices, when appropriate at the expense of yourself and people around you. The initiative is shouldering responsibility and briefly it is the choice and being prepared to the consequences of these choices and responsibilities. Initiative is an experience and it requires knowledge and experience. The results of everyone's initiative are not the same. At the right place and time, effective usage of it accelerates events and prevents waste of time. In management area, to take the initiative is a need undoubtedly. Of course, it is not correct to take the initiative and apply at every situation and condition. Initiative is a risk at the same time. In particular, initiatives not based on experience will result in negative.

As well as these, taking the initiative at specific intervals and different levels and then observing their results will also enhance your experience and expertise.

Initiative should be examined in four categories:

<u>Individual Initiative:</u> It refers to the initiative which is taken by an individual alone.

<u>Team Initiative:</u> It refers to the joint initiative of the whole team.

<u>Situational Initiative:</u> Refers to the initiative which varies depending on the varying condition.

<u>Positional Initiative:</u> It refers to the scope of initiative which varies according to the position.

Stability

Stability is to provide and maintain a certain order. Rather than literally expressing, I think it would be more effective to characterize it within the scope of the topic. In leadership and administratorship, stability can be presented in different contexts. However stability is the maintenance of the continuity of a particular situation, activity or qualification. So, why stability is important in management area? We will give place to different definitions to examine the stability better.

<u>Leader's Individual Stability</u>: Leader's own stability. It is concerned with the self-management, personality and characteristics and also every scope which is under influence of himself.

<u>Manager's Individual Stability</u>: If the manager is also a leader, definition of leader's individual stability is also valid for this purpose. If the manager is only a manager and does not show leadership qualities, then we can handle this scope as providing stability at every aspect of business life and personal life of the manager.

<u>Team Stability:</u> Is the stability that emphasizes the harmony of the team, their work, and the qualifications of the people in the team and the diversity of these properties.

<u>Managerial Stability:</u> Management is an understanding that can be applied to all areas. It also means forming chains of many people and providing control of these chains. Management contains order, discipline, and work activities in it within the scope of its application area. Stability of these activities with respect to the strategies which are implemented or not implemented (not implemented strategy is also a strategy) can be characterized as administrative stability. Is stability important? Yes, it is important. Is instability important? Yes, it is important too. Before I explain my statement, let me define stability:

<u>Absolute Stability:</u> Stability is flawless and doubtless in the absolute stability. There is no exception and it refers to a continuous stability arrangement without deviations.

Let's continue to the importance of stability. Is stability important? No, it is insignificant. Is instability important? No, it is insignificant. No matter how you think about stability and instability and how you apply, you cannot provide absolute stability. This is impossible under any circumstances. Hardly by means of a perfect machine and a seamless computing environment you may ensure it.

If you would ask me, stability is important, particularly in the management and implementation stages. However a realistic stability expectation and a realistic result have always been a pioneer for me. Of course, your perspective, comment, synthesis depends on you. As well as these, taking a stable stance is important not only in the management field but also in our daily lives.

<u>Taking a stable stance:</u> There is always stability in the decisions, ideas and applications of the effective leader. How consistent can be a leader who is contradicting himself? How can he provide stability? Even in this simple example, we can observe how important stability is. Again in this context, there is a point I want to add, but it needs to be understood better. Because usually due to loss in meaning, problems may occur. Even when you go wrong, do not lose your stability and keep your stance. Of course, this can lead to instability. My main issue that I want to focus on is the importance of the principles in stability. If you want stability, do not compromise your principles. If you have to do, check whether that decision shake the stability or not. Yes, we have actually expressed one more scope. "The importance of the principles in stability."

If we sum up, how you deal with stability and apply it are up to you. I have presented you the definition, scope and comments of stability. You can choose among them or continue with new insights and comments.

Practicalness

Effective leaders finish the job that take place in a field or scope. They conclude it and get the results. "Practicalness" is a responsibility, a qualification and a skill. It requires expertise and equipment. Practicalness is not an easy ability. Practicalness which is based on completion of a job whether it is easy or hard, heavy or light, simple or complex is a feature that usually belongs to effective leadership. It is a feature that we may encounter in the upper levels of leadership.

Why is practicalness important? Why cannot everyone be a practical one? Are you a practical person?

Let's assume that a responsibility or a work is given at any field. A long or short period of time is given. In this context, the main scope of practicalness is the process you get the responsibility, you finish the work and get the result. Consequently, only just finishing the work and getting the result is not important. It is a whole process from start to finish. At this point, the importance and difficult of work emerge. That is why, everyone cannot achieve this, every leader cannot achieve also, and only effective leaders can do. All titles in this book cover the issues that occur in this process. Consequently, this requires practicalness, experience, equipment, skill and knowledge.

Business Life and Private Life

The marching time jerks over our time and our life continuously. Our hours, our days, our years and our life pass immediately. Well, can we actually make use of these moments, seconds and times well? Do we know their value? Or throughout our whole life, do we always want more and more consistently? Are we grateful for everything? Do we appreciate that? Or do we provide that? What do we add ourselves? And what do we add to people around us? What do we steal from ourselves? Do we make concessions? Are we sacrificing all our lives for a few piece of paper? Or else, do we know the value of everything and give thanks and enjoy every moment that we live?

Every day we wake up and run to school, work ... For lots of hours we have worked and struggled for years ... All our efforts, for what? To be able to survive? Or to be more successful? Or to spend a more relaxed life? To be able to earn more money? More ... More ... More ... So, how are we now? Currently what do we not like? Well, when we get the better will everything be complete or will we ask even better the next day? Now answer them in just a few minutes or in a more suitable time question yourself. We confront "more" again. What could be more important than them? It is fully up to you ...

Let's talk about our work life and private life, are you a workaholic? Are you someone who likes to work? Do you work because you love working? Or because to be able to do what you love? Do you love your job? How much time do you spend for your private life? Do you neglect your family and environment? In particular, do you neglect yourself?

Business life is an inevitable necessity. Of course, if you do not have an inheritance or do not have someone to do your work, in the meantime different responsibilities will bring work. Business life often takes more time than the private life. Because the system is based on "more and more". At this point to love what you are doing is the most important principle. Of course it is not a valid statement that you cannot be successful if you do not like your job. Even if you regard your job just as a tool for the purposes in your life and isolate yourself in this regard, you have apprehended something.

In addition, if you have a very stressful job, do not like your job, you go to your job loathingly and look forward rush hour every day, then your life will be upside down just like a domino effect. Of course, we can come across exceptions as well. However, thinking a little bit on these problems and questions generally and defining our own rights and wrongs and setting off according to them are "more" important than the work that we do now. When it comes to private life, it is something more important and effective than work life. If problems exist in our private lives, blasting away and resolving these problems and deficiencies are very important. Private life of the effective leader is based on solid foundations, effective leader is the one who can establish the balance between work and private life ideally. In general, weekly, monthly or for a special time interval that you define, question your life shortly. Evaluate both positive and negative aspects of yourself, things you did, do and will do. If you want it to be permanent, then keep a diary. Your life is very important, care your every moment, know its value and add value. The most important achievement is things you leave behind, your experiences and things other people have experienced because of you.

Reputation Management

Reputation is a concept word meaning of which corresponds to dignity, respect and prestige. As well as creating reputation, protecting, enhancing and managing it are also important. If we examine meanings of these concepts:

<u>Creating reputation:</u> To be recognized in a particular environment. This recognition is created by the help of specific scopes and stages. This covers activities which were done and have been done within the formation.

<u>Enhancing Reputation:</u> Moving the existing reputation to better, widening it. This development is only possible by protecting the existing reputation and adding to the available one.

<u>Protecting Reputation:</u> It is to protect the existing reputation. Not harming the available reputation and protecting it.

<u>Reputation Management:</u> Reputation management encompasses building the reputation, enhancing the reputation and protecting the reputation. Reputation management cannot be applied by many leaders. Many of them are victims of their ambitions and megalomaniac

ideas and cannot perform the basis of reputation management. In addition to these, individuals who forget leadership principles because of their struggle to glorify their reputation and pay no attention to their team, environment and relations are typical examples of moving away from effective leadership qualities.

The most effective reputation is being loyal to yourself and your environment, not losing the feeling of gratitude and refraining from self-praise. Ensuring this is difficult because the environment is a competitive environment. At this point, people who internalize and apply it would provide a real reputation.

Acceptance Policy

People do not always accept facts because actually there are not always positive or negative factors at stake. In this context, facts have the power to destroy hopes, prospects and expectations or to the contrary. The concept that we qualify as fact is actually the real life itself, a reflection of this word. Escaping from the facts can be interpreted as escaping from the consequences of life or life itself, and of course fact and factuality words can lead to different interpretations in different areas and scopes. Some use philosophical, some ideological, and some dictionary definition and make definitions, comments and adaptations.

In our daily lives we cannot accept everything as it is. We may deny contrary effects and do not want to accept opposite opinions. Sometimes in a good and sometimes in a bad sense; These criticisms can lead to sometimes positive and sometimes negative consequences. As well as these, accepting or not accepting and criticizing ourselves when we make mistake gain importance at this point.

In leadership and administratorship, this scope can be applied in almost every field. In particular, accepting his own mistakes completely affects the success for the person who is manager or leader. Moreover this is not limited only to the effect on success and leads to many results in various fields such as efficiency, order between activities and so on. In fact, issues which are accepted or not accepted are not confined to the manager only. Let us explain the functional acceptance principle by means of a simple example. For example, from managers to assistants, secretaries or janitors, namely everyone in the workplace must be aware of their own position and task, also they need to accept them. If they do not accept their work or involved in different tasks unnecessarily, there may occur jealousy and restlessness in the company.

We should not accept everything in our lives, every truth is not acceptable. Every mistake is not, as well. That is important to behave as required when it is necessary. This will be shaped based on you, your road map, your personal characteristics, your leadership skills and other skills that you have.

As well as these, you can reject something inside yourself while admitting it at outside or vice versa. In the meantime, it can be clear that you have questioned yourself or you have a different strategic structure.

Essence of the matter is honesty, strategy and being well-equipped personally. At least two of these three principles directly reflect your level of acceptance. So, which two of these reflect you better, what do you think? Which factors restrict or expand your ability to gain acceptance?

Permanence

Throughout our life, we take place in many environments and tasks. So, how permanent are we in the meantime? How permanent is the things that we have done? Or is it important for you to be permanent?

If we handle the issue as leadership based, the importance of leaving an impression is undoubtedly clear. At every step of the leadership, there is adding something to someone else's life. Being permanent has variable importance among leaders. Each leader's own personal structure and decision determines the level of his permanence. However, most of the permanent leaders are effective leaders because being permanent especially from generation to generation is not something that every leader can do. Being permanent is to be based on solid foundations, to leave impression, to be dominant, different and special.

Open Door and Closed Door Policies

As a leader and manager your door should be open to everyone because you're the brain of all your employees. However, keeping your door always open can affect you negative by psychologically, physically, and functionally. During the intense pace, there may be things that you need to do, you may want to rest your head, you may want to give your team the message that you do not want to be disturbed ... Of course, these are all normal. You're the brain of the team, you need to take good care of yourself. Working continuously does not mean that working efficiently, managing your time well will improve your efficiency.

If we get to the closed door policy, this policy serves many purposes, not for only one purpose, which are;

- Authority
- Personal Efficiency
- Team Efficiency
- Message

<u>Authority</u>: You should not lose your authority in the team. This can result in disaster. Therefore, by applying this policy occasionally, you can keep this dynamism active. As well as these, perceiving the closed door policy simply as shutting the door and creeping into your own skin is totally wrong. Here the objective is, occasionally making understand to your team and your environment that you have the authority.

<u>Personal Efficiency:</u> In order to make yourself more efficient, relax and be alone with yourself, you can apply this policy.

<u>Team Efficiency:</u> You can ensure the overall efficiency of your team and emphasize that everyone is separate individuals and show different personal abilities and talents. When these are united, team spirit reveals and team work is not possible without individual effort.

<u>Message</u>: By means of what you do, what you say, which policy you prefer, you give messages to your team and others from different aspects. This policy is located as one of the multiple messages. Additionally, you can arrange the people who enter the room. By this way, you can shift unnecessary or less important people and groups to later on (especially when your time is limited).

Do not forget that the era of oppressor managers has closed. Now, today and in the future, it will be exception to see this type of managers. We already know that an understanding like that cannot be in a continuous manner, but do not forget that you have undertaken the heaviest burden and you are the most responsible one at the last possible moment. Of course, everyone likes chatting and having break but this should never bring with laziness and loss of authority.

In summary, using the closed door policy when necessary is an advantage for you. However if you apply this policy when it is not necessary, then you will observe easily that others perspective about your authority, your leadership and change immediately and getting rid of this negativity is not as easy as you think.

Do not be an unapproachable manager, you are there because you are the source of fast and effective solution. If it is difficult to reach you (especially for your team) it can also be difficult to put things right. If we come to the conclusion, you need to balance the closed door policy and open door policy. You are the one to establish this balance.

Steering Your Career

Career is a concept which is essentially effective in many areas especially at business life and have different degrees of importance on the lives of people. Career can create different meanings and connotations for everyone. For this reason, everyone has different career goals, since everyone's talents, abilities, lifestyle, business objective, personal characteristics are different.

Being developmental/ developmental leadership, strategy/ strategy in leadership are the topics related with career.

Indeed, self-improvement and working for a better career opportunity is important in terms of the applied strategy and defined way.

We can discuss about coaching in leadership within the scope of career consultants, experts, and individual developers. Of course, these people carry on their business by guiding, leading and supporting others. However career goals, even goals should not be determined by someone else. Determination of your goals by someone else is a very silly situation. Such an understanding cannot be accepted. If you will be the one who will get the results from the implementation, then you should conduct the implementation and make the selection. Because this way, preferences, career, and your life are yours. External factors can just give idea or support for shaping the goals that you have chosen.

If you ask me, there is not certain steps and rules in determining and shaping your career. You will determine it in compliance with your own direction. Choosing activities such as reading books, watching movies, and chatting with different people on this subject may be supportive to conduct selection, synthesis and implementation about defining goals.

If you are going to ask what is the most important thing at determining your career, the answer is clear. Knowing yourself. We should emphasize it insistently because knowing yourself is basic. If there are deficiencies in this basic, then even in the lightest earthquake, steps will be destroyed. Another reason for me to address this issue is in this regard there are serious shortcomings today. People synthesize their own preferences and analyses on others and then transfer these ones to themselves. So that, they can see the different characters in their own character. They may not be able to create their own characters.

Together with these, they may be condemned to unconsciously conduct activities and work which are out of their field of interests, because they have not noticed and defined their wishes and skills throughout their life. This is a very serious matter and it must be internalized.

A solution should be found without facing disaster. What matters is life, it is a continuum of lifelong. Regardless of his position in this process, individual should be aware of this. In fact, whether he is fifteen years old or fifty-five years old, this can and should be converted into profits. Actually career is not limited to being written on paper? Positive and negative situations that it brings along are at a serious level. Of course, when it is noticed ...

Get to know yourself, discover your skills, address your main interest areas, and definitely apply your dominant and recessive skills. First you can define side interest areas which are shaped around a main area of interest. However, during the developing process, enlarge your main and side interest areas. Each interest area will add you a different world. Over the time, you will observe that your perspective, knowledge, skills, efficiency, effectiveness and career have been improved. In this context, we can say that, your career may influence everything in your life and also may be affected from everything.

Charisma

Usually the qualification which is defined as a leadership quality is expressed to be due to the charisma. Charisma is also used as impressiveness. Charisma is a qualification in itself. Today after all, application of charisma is possible at certain levels thanks to the researches and knowledge on this area. More importantly, the qualification that the individual has is essential. If this is developed, impressiveness would be fully realized. Leadership,because of this, has been considered as an art of impressiveness. But this approach has lost its validity. Today and in the future, leadership understanding that depends on only charisma has been disappearing. Because charisma is just like a hollow piano. It consists of keys and only has an appearance. Therefore, it cannot make sound. Particularly intellectual leaders whom will emerge more as I guess have no charisma. While intellectual leaders take place in theory and guiding, charismatic leaders can take place in practice. It is almost like puppeteer-puppet relationship. Puppeteer guides but puppet is in view and application. In this context, the puppeteer can be exemplified as intellectual leader and the puppet can be exemplified as charismatic leader. However at this point we only observe the insignificance of the charismatic leadership. In leadership communication, persuasive skill and dominance are important. We have inspected this topic in detail. Charisma is also important in this context. However in the past, individuals who do not demonstrate impressive and persuasive features were not called as leaders. Now, especially in this context, I argue that people who do not demonstrate impressive and persuasive features can also be leaders but their leadership is confined to intellectual leadership.

As we will mention in the leadership steps, the first step of leadership is being a model and exhibiting activities which will be pioneer. So when a person displays a behavior which sets another person an example or leaves a mark on him, then that person is at the first step of leadership. This is a kind of impressiveness. In this regard, confusion should be eliminated. Behaviors which leave a mark are directly or indirectly related with impressiveness.

If we are to pick up the threads, leadership and administratorship do not depend on just charisma only. Charisma is part of the required properties. In this context, the only difference is the intellectual leadership. In the essence of this issue, fascinating feature in leadership and administratorship is important. However fascinating feature alone will lose its sufficiency both at present and in the future.

Concept - Word

Concept is the structure that explains general design of objects, events, definitions and scopes. It is composed of letters, syllables, and words and makes sense. While words can also be a concept; concept can also be a word at the same time. But concept is a more powerful statement. Leadership, management and administration are both word and concept. But in respect to scopes, it is more accurate to characterize as concept. Another definition of the concept from a different perspective is being abstractness. At this point leadership, management and administration are abstract but they are concrete with regard to their implementation. I will discuss this relationship under the heading "Abstract-Concrete Understanding" in the following pages.

To repeat, definitions of leadership, management and administration are open ended and they are not fixed,since their scopes are deep and they are handled at different formats. In general terms, basic features can be described and definitions can be made within this context.

Gain

If you are the only winner side in leadership and management, do you think that you really win? In these two concepts, there is no "me", there is "we". So, if you are the only person who wins in an activity, then which role your team or other person have played or playing?

Winning is not only in the material sense, definitely you gain in return of any endeavor. You will either gain experience or earn success or you receive something in return or by losing you gain experience again.

In the basis of leadership and administratorship, there must be mutual gain. We can explain these parties as follows:

- Gain between team, leader and manager.
- Gain between team, leader, manager and counter party.

Gain between team, leader and manager.

- If you only gain there must be a deficiency and you should question your leadership or administratorship.

- Likewise if the other person only gains, there must be a fault, hence you should question yourself.

- If both parties lose, then you should question your team and yourself whom manage or lead this team.

- If both you and your team gain, it means you have demonstrated a correct development.

- Gain between team, leader, manager and counter party

- If the team, leader and manager gain, counter party loses, developmental aspect is positive and does not cause problem, then by establishing control, process can continue.

- If the team, leader and manager lose and counter party gains, a situation assessment should be conducted and mistakes and shortcomings should be compensated and also team inquiry should be done. In accordance with the responsibility of leader / manager, personal and team shortcomings should be reviewed.

- If both sides lose, team, leader and manager should question themselves and they should design the next activity so as to turn it into advantage. As well as these, experience which is brought by losing should be noticed. If this awareness is ensured, lost issue will become gain.

- If both sides gain, it means that you are proceeding in an efficient and productive manner. However , if you do not always have a grip on the issue, balance may become reversed. Therefore, do not allow double-sided earnings to change your layout and principles.

One of the foundations of gain-based leadership and administratorship is giving an opportunity to life. If we examine this issue a little bit more;

Giving a chance to the team to make mistake may be more useful than explaining these mistakes to them. For them, being aware of these mistakes will be more effective than trying to create awareness about them. If you consistently apply this strategy, after a while you will notice that it does not work. The most effective approach is ensuring balance between these two. It is necessary to create necessary opportunities and provide necessary ground when required.

When the issue is the mistake of leader or manager, this is very different from the other. It is necessary for you to obtain individual experience and after a certain stage you need to minimize the mistakes. Since your team will increase in number day by day,consequently your responsibilities will increase and the impact of your error rate will have negative effect on your team.

Coach

As we all know coach has two meanings. One of these meanings is a comfortable bus used to take groups of people on long journeys. The other meaning is the one that we will discourse on now.

Coach, mentor and leader are the concepts which are often confused. Today, even many leaders or managers are unaware of the differences between them. I believe that it is necessary to clarify this matter first.

Mentor: while it means directing and guiding, leader means individual who leads and implements this qualification at various stages.

Coach-esque leader: It corresponds to coach-leader or coaching based leadership. Coach has a similar meaning but it is an attribution that includes different scopes.

Coach has the duty to guide and train any person or society. Yet it is not expected from him to be expert on this training or it is not expected from him to carry out only training duty. Coaching is the sharing of mutual experiences and ideas in order to achieve agreed bilateral results.

Who can be a coach?

People who are open to mutual sharing and exchange of ideas and experiences and have training qualification can be a coach. Coaches do not have to show leadership qualities. Coaches do not have to be experts or well-equipped. However, coaches have better training quality, qualification, capacity, experience and equipment than their counter party within mutual exchange of experiences and ideas.

Condition

What is condition?

Condition is presenting the implemented activity as a result of individual's own capacity. We usually encounter condition in sport, but condition takes place in every area at different basis. In music within the context of condition, instruments exercises, repertoire repetition, note studies can be given as examples. When we look at our daily lives, answers to the questions such as how many tasks we complete, how our performance can be described as condition. If we are to give an example about housework, in how much time how much work you do, how well your performance are depend on your condition.

Condition in leadership and administration is divided into two parts as individual and team:

Individual Condition: How well you work individually, efficiency rate of this time period, your performance in your daily life and work life

are evaluated under the scope of individual condition.

<u>Team Condition:</u> It can be expressed as the individual condition of the people on your team together with the total condition created by the entire team.

Effective condition is not obtained by working very hard. Active condition is obtaining maximum efficiency and success at minimum time. It also reveals the direct relationship between the condition and success. As condition increases, success increases. At this point, we can say that condition and success are directly proportional.

Increasing condition is possible by means of practice not theory. By practicing and implementation you can increase your condition. The more and frequent you practice, the more you will have condition. At this point we can say that, practice and condition are directly proportional.

Do not work hard, work efficiently. Do not run so much, run effectively. Do not rest so much, rest as much as you get tired. Try to carry your condition a step forward at every field. Remember that the condition that you have is what you are able to do, your capacity is much higher than that.

Coordination

In leadership and administratorship, coordination between people, management, activities, orders, team and leader, team and counter party, senior management and units are very important. If you conduct an activity without providing coordination, you will always notice that something is missing and also you may not make the activity efficient.

So, How to ensure coordination? First of all, you need to know that coordination has many types. Unilateral coordination, bilateral coordination, partial coordination, main coordination, dominant coordination. Let's have a look at them.

<u>Unilateral Coordination:</u> It refers to individual's own coordination and the coordination with counter person. As well, the coordination of the team with the leader can be an example to this.

<u>Bilateral Coordination:</u> It is interpersonal or inter-unit coordination. Coordination between the senior management and unit, team and leader are examples of this coordination type.

Partial Coordination: Partiality of multiple coordination in certain areas.

Main Coordination: Is concentrating on the outline and main sections of the coordination. Here coordination is fully ensured about relationship and topics which are within the scope of activities and people.

Dominant Coordination: Refers to complete and precise dominance of coordination. They act almost like a flawless machines compatible with each other. This also makes it easier to solve many problems, success, efficiency and consistency are achieved in this way.

Crisis Management

In our daily lives, business lives, just in everywhere at every moment we can face crisis. As crisis management plays a very significant role in many companies, it is very important in our daily lives meantime.

Although they have many common denominator, I think that crisis management in our daily lives and crisis management in our business lives should be handled separately.

If we look at the crises in our daily lives, we may encounter many examples. (A short reminder: Crisis is not only in the material sense.) We constantly face with ups and downs by nature of our lives. We have many troubles, unsolvable results, unstable situations. So as to overcome them, some experience, a little knowledge, and a little management are needed. We have to move forward with firm steps to deal with crisis management. At the first step, being prepared to crisis, thinking about the problems that may come at any moment, designing and producing solutions are the necessary actions. So, what if you are not prepared to crisis and have no countermeasure? Then you need to start by recognizing, defining and understanding the crisis. How the crisis affects your life? What is the size of crisis? What kind of crisis is it? If you understand the crisis first, then you can proceed with more confidently.

Let's say you have understood the crisis, what should you do then? You must take control of the crisis. You should exhibit the necessary determination, and though just barely bring the crisis under control. If you have difficulties when taking control of the crisis, according to the condition of the subject and activity, you should receive support from others. But this should not cause loss of time. You should immediately identify key tools or people and carry into action. After taking control of the crisis, you will see that everything becomes easier, and then hit the road to resolve the crisis. In this process, no matter what happens, do not lose your commitment and remember to use the time well. At the time you neglect the crisis, aftershock crises may come in succession and you may severely be affected from them. You can take a little breath after the crisis come to a solution. Be careful, I did not say a deep breath because, we have just come to the important point. Question yourself, question why the crisis has developed, its causes and effects. Internalize the results. If you have not taken countermeasures, take lesson from this. If you took countermeasures, then why did the crisis happen? Did not you taken sufficient countermeasures? Or is there a deficiency elsewhere? Question it, internalize and take lessons. Have you done? Now you can take a deep breath ...

Let's talk about crisis management in our business and administratorship lives. In general terms, crisis management can be explained in two ways. Ongoing crisis about natural disasters and the company. Actually, natural disasters are crises that may happen at any time. We may encounter many problems such as fire, earthquake, flood etc. In fact, natural disasters are in our daily life crises. Taking precaution is the first action to protect against natural disasters. Of course sometimes unavoidable disasters may happen. At that time, crisis management should come into play. As for the crises in companies, we encounter many reasons. Internal and external factors, market value, political situation, the ups and downs are among the reasons that pave the way for crisis. Undoubtedly these variations make crisis management more challenging. However, taking the right steps will enable to overcome the crisis. First step: No matter at which situation you are, make sure that you do crisis planning. At this step, no matter how clever, how experienced, how good a manager you are, you must necessarily act as a leader. You should get your team's opinion because two heads are better than one and details that you can overlook during crisis planning can lead directly or indirectly to the crisis. Therefore when doing crisis planning, do it with your team, not alone. The scope of this plan must be based on conditions and capacity of your business or your company. For example, you can create a comprehensive crisis plan for computer data backup or you can create a superficial plan. If you have a computer software company then your scope will be different and if you are in commercial business then your scope will be different as well. Depending on your time period, you can give place to the events that have low probability. For example, if you are at a location where probability of an earthquake occurrence is very low, then you can postpone earthquake plans or give place to them in the background. As well as these, defining a crisis controller will reveal all this dynamism. According to potential, you can shift this duty for specific time period within the team. When you have done these at the first step, you can take a little breath. When you identify key people during the crisis, collect the necessary information and guarantee yourself, your company and your team, you can take a deep breath. Let's say you've applied them, but still a crisis occurred. Be assured that you will overcome this crisis more effectively, because you have already conducted a specific study. Furthermore, you may encounter a completely different crisis to which you did not give place in your crisis plan. In the meantime, let me give you a few tips and by this way you will overcome any possible crisis that you may confront. First, let's repeat the steps of the crisis:

1. Doing Crisis Planning
2. Recognizing and Identifying Crisis
3. Taking Control of Crisis
4. Solving Crisis
5. Taking Lesson from Crisis

Let's talk about basic tips that will save you:

- Stability
- Consistency

- Patience
- Using time well, doing the necessary on time
- Being honest and trustworthy
- Not abandoning leadership qualification and principles
- Overcoming with the team, not alone

If you accept these basics, internalize steps and apply them, no crisis can beat you in your daily and business life ...

Leadership Steps

Leadership steps can vary with respect to individuals, theories or forms of expressions. I prefer to express it at five steps and explain leadership at this direction. If we look at these steps,

1. Monotonic Leader

2. Field Leader

3. Ambient Leader

4. Multiple Leader

5. Effective Leader

1. <u>Monotonic Leader:</u> A leader who has served as a model for a few issue throughout his life, only applied the first step of leadership with little guiding practices and did not do more than a few activities.

2. <u>Field Leader:</u> A leader who has knowledge only in specific areas, led in certain fields, dominant on specific topics.

3. <u>Ambient Leader:</u> A leader who becomes pioneer in the environment that he enters and does not limited to specific areas.

4. <u>Multiple Leader:</u> A leader who has in-depth knowledge in many subjects, shows leadership qualities in many areas and dominates issues and leadership.

5. <u>Effective Leader:</u> A leader who can lead all subjects, dominates all matters, takes the lead in every profession, every study group and other activities and has experience and expertise of many areas.

In general, short descriptions of the steps are in this manner. So, at which step are you?

These steps are not steps to be skipped or to be quickly passed. The speed that I meant is not the only in the sense of time, climbing without firm foundation and without completion of tasks in each step can be given as examples. Consequently, these steps can be completed in a few years or during a lifetime as well ...

Climbing steps firmly is the essential matter. No leader can reach the third step without climbing the first or second step. If an individual reaches that step, then for whom or for what that leadership understanding is? Since each step cannot be realized or developed without the previous one. Eventually many factors especially individual effort, skill, talent, intelligence, perseverance and patience play role. The first and most important thing that the leader will do is knowing himself and being able to lead himself. For an individual who is not aware of himself or is not able to lead himself, being leader to others is a weak possibility. After realizing these, leader will begin from the first step.

In fact, most people around us is at the first step or have just completed the first step. Although first step is the most simple step, many people are unconsciously aware of this step. Awareness begins at the second stage by self-improvement. Not forget that, leadership is a qualification. And many people has this qualification. To reveal it and make additions on it are merit. People who realize this will be on the top of leaders and leadership understanding which are confined to qualification only. If we return to the beginning we should first know ourselves and lead ourselves, recognize steps, internalize their features and then dominate these steps and consequently climb up these steps with a firm and strong leadership understanding.

Leadership and Politics

Politics is an important issue that can influence many issues and also can be easily influenced by many issues in our daily lives. Also, leadership is the main source of politics and politicians. The reason for the vast influence and coverage of politics and coverage, is based upon leadership qualities and leading politicians. A politician who is not a leader cannot succeed, even if he succeed, it would be deficient. However, if we internalize it, different examples may emerge of course. For example, a party, leader of which does not have leadership qualities, can rise to main opposition or power. The main issue to be considered is the situation that arises as a result of the characteristics of leaders and consultants within the party. At this condition, leadership qualification is ahead again. When you have a look at different and extreme examples, you will be able to make these observations especially in politics.

Of course, every leader in politics is not an effective leader. That is why the political situation of each country varies. There is no doubt that if the person who governs the country is an effective leader, then generally the country will make progress.

Leadership and politics complement each other, both need each other and also both cover each other. Politicians and leaders are required to raise awareness and internalize this awareness.

Satisfaction

Have a look around yourself. Where are you, what are you doing, why are you here? Do you complain about being here or do you like it? Let's say you are satisfied to be here but are you satisfied with your life? Life is like a rapidly progressing process and emotions in this process take place at a very important part of our lives. If we express the feeling of satisfaction, it is within the scope of gratitude and content.

Do we satisfied with what we do, our relationships, our business lives, our private lives, shortly anything in our lives, or not? So, what does it bring us? How does it affect us?

If we examine the sense of satisfaction in two scopes:

<u>Feeling Satisfaction:</u> It refers to doing something which satisfies the person or group and counter person or group does something which creates satisfaction at person or group. Self-recognition is essential.

<u>Bringing Satisfaction:</u> It refers to bringing satisfaction by the person or group to counter party. Here, rather than individual, counter party is essential.

In general, the feeling of satisfaction, brings along contentment and gratitude concepts. This will affect the peace of mind and performed activities in daily life. If you have dissatisfaction about yourself, your own life or your environment, start from yourself and if counter party has dissatisfaction about any issue start from questioning yourself again and then your counter party. In particular, it is important to satisfy the counter party in business relations. If you satisfy the counter party with the right strategic moves, you will definitely get a positive return in the future. At this point, it can be stated that the feeling of satisfaction actually plays an important role in the spiritual sense and understanding this will result in positive changes.

Mission

Mission is a borrowed word in Turkish like the word vision. It also means purpose or duty, but particularly in management we use the word mission. Since, as well as its word meaning, it refers to foundation principles and existence justifications. In order to be understood easily, it may be formed by asking questions. Ask yourself questions based on the company's policy, and responses to these questions will help you to explain your mission.

I think, a company / organization which does not have a mission is almost like a person who does not know himself. How can a person who does not know himself go ahead? As I mentioned repeatedly, knowing yourself is the basis of everything. A person or an organization which does not know himself or itself does not have the necessary qualification to advance. In this context, a leader or a manager with mission is as important as in the management.

Having a mission is also necessary for the vision. Having vision without having mission is like starting to run without crawling.

This issue which is important in management life is also important in our daily lives. An individual who has principles and mission will be more effective in his environment. In this context, a good understanding and practicing of mission is needed.

Self-Control

Can we dominate ourselves? When we see a dessert, want expensive cars, men see beautiful woman, women see handsome men ... Can we hold our horses? Is money taking over our soul?

In fact, this issue is also included in the scope of self-management and self-dominance. When self is uncontrolled, it can lead to very serious problems. Therefore, we have to control ourselves, we should not allow ourselves not to dominate over us so as to spend more successful, happier, and better life.

The same point is at issue for leaders and managers. After all, leaders and managers are also human beings. Especially leaders and managers need to be more controlled especially at topics such as self-control, self-management, personal dominance and self. I would like to remind that individual should start with his own leadership and control. As well as these, if we talk about the scope of leadership and administration, being overwhelmed by ambition of money and success would derail us from the way of effective leadership. At this point we observe the importance of self-control. After all, in the advanced stages of being uncontrolled, sickly problems and difficulties will come along. Therefore, no matter who or no matter what happens, individuals who cannot control his self shall receive aid or exert himself.

Point Shot

Every step and every action in leadership and management carries great significance. Even with a single move you can configure everything or destroy everything. To give an example about time management, one minute thinking can supersede hours of working. In this context, a move can save you from making several moves. Well, what should be this move and how should be it? This move is point shot. Point shot is usually the critical point, the central move of the targets towards solution. Point shot can turn a negative situation into a positive situation, failure to success, bankruptcy to profit but it certainly depends on the move made. This move can convert this effect into failure, bankruptcy and negativity as well.

Effective leaders make the point shot best. The timing of the point shot is also very important. At a time making a point shot when it is not needed or needed little is meaningless and at the same time it is a wrong move as well. Making the point shot in an effective way depends on whether the leader is effective. Point shot is not tied to a single achievement. It needs to all principles of effective leadership. This demonstrates that apart from effective leaders no one can make a good point shot. As well as these, when point shot is made in a single scope and depending on the strategy of that scope, an individual who is expert and well-equipped on this field can do this, regardless of effective leader qualification. In general terms, effective leader is the person who makes the point shot best in every field and scope.

Our Priorities

We all have priorities. Voluntary or involuntary, controlled or uncontrolled we rank our priorities. To determine our priorities well is among the main factors to regulate our lives in line with our own free will. So, how do you set your priorities?

Choosing your priorities well in management and leadership will make you more successful and effective. It is entirely related with you, your understanding, and your experience. Interchanging the first one and the second one in your priority list may even lead to serious changes. Consequently, your priorities in every area of your life represent you and affect you directly. Therefore, there is no steps to follow when ordering your priorities or defining their urgencies. These factors are determined by your mindset and your environment.

By giving place to your priorities, you can relax and as you complete your list you will reach your goal. Target is yours, path is yours, life is yours, it is none of my business.

Self-Management

Self-management is the most important management type. Everything begins with managing yourself good. Effective leadership is realized with the supportive factor of self-management.

So, what is self-management? It is recognizing, managing and dynamizing individual's own abilities, perception abilities, learning principles, feelings, senses and in short, everything connected with himself.

Self-management is a form of personal domination. It is the ability of individual to control and dominate qualifications about himself and related with himself. If leader and manager have dominance on self-management, then much more robust and efficient steps are taken.

Concepts such as self-confidence, self-esteem, self-motivation are directly in scope of self-management. Individual's perception, impressionistic aspects, physical ownership, health status, personality and characteristics, how individual defines himself are also in self-management.

The first and most important step of self-management is knowing yourself, recognizing all kinds of requirements and features of yourself and observing yourself. If this is done in a healthy way then the domination will come. Dominance of self-management in all areas consists of several steps. Weak dominance, settled dominance, basic dominance, strong dominance and full dominance.

These steps are related with the individual himself and how he performs the self-management. Being on the top of these steps will facilitate being effective and efficient for managers and leaders.

Plan

Are you a planned one? Do you plan? Do you abide by your plan? Is plan important for you? Is plan a success or a tool for accessing to success?

There are planned and unplanned people around us. It is interesting that in the way to be successful, being planned or not does not have a distinctive feature certainly.

Plan is arrangement of a specific period of time, situation and goal and division of it into expressions. Being planned, making effective plans and adhering to that plan is not the reason for success but is an inevitable necessity of effective leadership. Because effective leaders do not leave their business to chance and they do not act in an unplanned and unscheduled way. Only exceptional people succeed in an unplanned manner. Without doubt, they are outside the scope of an effective leadership.

Uncovering the Potential and Managing the Potential Change

If we define the potential within the subject that we handle, it is the owned accumulation that have emerged or undisclosed.

When individual reveal his potential, he also knows himself well. This is the case in all areas of life. Individual who does not know himself well cannot comprehend his own potential and cannot reach to the highest level of his potential.

If we define the potential as the possessed competences and consider it as a whole, then we can explain the potential by levels. Let's consider these levels in three ways:

1. <u>Low Potential:</u> Low potential is the potential level which arises without any effort in a usual manner.

2. <u>Medium Potential:</u> Medium potential arises by means of showing a certain level of effort and adding to the ordinary potential level.

3. <u>High Potential:</u> High potential arises by means of exerting efforts at highest level and points out the highest level of the potential.

The whole potential comes from innate. Providing, maintaining and enhancing this whole ideally still depends on the people's will and effort.

Exceeding the potential or exhibiting a performance over the potential are beyond the depth of most people. People who recognizes and focuses on their potential and skills well are usually effective leaders.

Potential levels of any conducted activity will determine the nature and result of those activities. Therefore working to know, understand, enhance and activate the potential well is also important in management strategy.

Enhancing the potential and working to climbing up to the high potential level also overlap with developmental leadership. However, as well as enhancing the potential, maintaining it is equally important. In my opinion, maintaining the potential is even more difficult than enhancing it. Maintaining potential is based on continuity, dominance, experience and competence. Also, reducing the potential in a controlled way is important under this topic. Here is the relationship between potential levels:

Reducing Potential Controlledly > Maintaining Potential > Enhancing Potential

Reducing the potential controlledly may seem nonsense and you may say that what is the reason to reduce potential to lower level. Here the fundamental point is to manage control and change of potential. Fluctuations and changes between the potential levels are structures difficult to control. As a result of enhancing potential, it may reach to the highest level in an uncontrolled way. Maintaining that level is the indicative of domination on that level. Enhancing potential and reducing potential controllably are based on total dominance and management over the potential. An individual who manages the potential and changes in these levels can go beyond the potential.

Project Management

Project is a draft which is designed at any point. Terminologically, project means drawing in terms of architecture and construction, and it also means scientific work draft which is decided to be realized in terms of management.

Project that we have envisioned in management field is a concept mostly based on management, developmental leadership, innovative, profit-oriented or strategically-directed.

Project management is the management of the draft in question. If we examine the project management in four main phases:

<u>Identification:</u> It refers to identification of the purpose, obligations, objectives, expectations and things to be done. It is the preparation to start.

<u>First Action</u>: It refers to the implementation of the identification, first application, first configuration and beginning of the project. It is the initial phase.

<u>Progress</u>: It refers to the development and consolidation of the draft which has been implemented. Also in

this phase project starts to acquire qualification. It is the qualifying phase for practice synthesis.

Finalization: It represents gaining result and reaching conclusion for the implementation phase. It is the last stage.

Project managers have the ability to obtain both success and failure, bring a new perspective to the management understanding, provide and developing dynamism and enable leaders to be both effective and ordinary.

Radical Leadership

Radical means fundamental and foundation. Radical changes mean substantial and fundamental change. Radical leadership, close to this meaning, shapes in the frame of sharp maneuvers and decisions.

At a certain level, radical leadership is covered within effective leadership. This level depends on the requirements during decision. Substantial change makes sense when applied as needed. That time is the time when effective leader prefers.

Due to its sharp stance, radical leadership creates very serious impact at a time when change is necessary. If it is applied when not necessary, it can result in disaster and also it can give better results than the current situation as well. This difference occurs depending on whether the leader is an effective leader or he is at the top of leadership stages.

Risk Taking

Have you ever taken risk in your life? Have you ever performed an action by taking the risk? In some cases, risk taking is inevitable and in other cases it is a concept based on individual preferences. In a sense, we confront risk taking at setting priorities and getting results. That states the likelihood of risk and also it states that risk does not express certainty.

Taking risk gives result depending on expertise, equipment, strategy, preferences, internal and external factors, and environmental factors. The possibility of win or lost at the end of the risk that you have taken gains meaning eventually.

Risk preferences in management and administration fields are of major significance. Even as a result of the taken risk, business can collapse or be saved from collapsing. Of course, luck factor also plays a part in risk taking. At this point, if it is necessary to introduce the rapid decision-making mechanism and time is limited, then intuition should be used in terms of intuitive leadership to make a decision. On the other hand, leaders who do not want to leave their business to chance activate strategic thinking and crisis management. However, from these two aspects, the two most important issue that should be in common is having another plan. Having plan B, plan C and even plan D will enable to reduce the nuisance during the risk taking process. Risk taking that has no guarantee detracts from effective leadership and does not mean anything at all.

Spiritual Leadership

All of us have inner voice. We observe that we think, we decide, we act based on our intuition and our feelings sometimes come to the forefront and outshine our logic. Spirit, intuition, feelings ... Whether you explain it by the help of religion or theory or whether you deny or believe. These are phenomena that affect us throughout our lives and are affected from the things that our lives have brought. Even if we go one step further, our soul live not only between birth and death, but also after death. I leave the investigation, reviews and preferences of this matter to you.

Without rambling around the subject, let's continue to leadership and its intersection with our subject which is our essential point. Inner voice, feeling or whatever you call it that everyone has affected the leader and leader's decisions. Some leaders act completely logical, some completely intuitive and some take advantage of both. At this point, it is necessary to discipline the brain and the feelings. It is necessary to establish, develop, consolidate a balance between these two and project this balance onto the life. By means of this intersection, we can say that only one definition for leadership is not sufficient and every leader has different variations in themselves and these selections lead to leaders and how leaders apply these qualifications. Every leader has faith, beliefs, thoughts, feelings at different levels. As a result of conducting researches based upon this fact, concluding that efficient leaders are faithful or inefficient leaders are faithless has no benefit and also contrary to effective leadership philosophy. Because this is an individual preference and success cannot be limited only to this. However and of course, intuition, feeling and spirit are among the factors affecting the leadership and success.

Health Management

In our lives, we have plans, desires, activities, things that we have been doing and things that we will do. In order to realize them we need a few basic and several general factors. What do you think about these basic and general factors? Of course, there may be different answers. Undoubtedly one of the basic factors that will not change is health. What can you do without health?

Health gathers everybody together under the same roof and is involved in every scope. We cannot generalize that successful people are the people who care about their health. However we can do it about effective leaders. Effective leaders pay attention to their health, care about it, and give priority to health. Even if we make a more general assessment, wise people are the people who pay attention to their health. Health is among continuities which have importance for them. Well, do you care about your health? Do you eat healthily? Do you do sports? Do you know the value of your life?

In many of the written resources about leadership and administratorship, you cannot find health management.

However I repeatedly express the necessity of this management and state that it is necessary for everyone to know that.

How does health management realize? Is health something manageable? Health is absolutely manageable. Of course, apart from accidents and exceptional results. As I always specify, the first condition to manage health is knowing yourself. The next step after knowing yourself is looking at your potential and involving in researches about health. Also you should not believe in all sorts of information, make a synthesis of researches and more importantly adapt this synthesis to yourself. This is not something that will come true at a moment, it is a process. It is also necessary to get results in short and long term by reducing this process to minimum.

Leadership of Virtual Teams

In constantly evolving competitive environment, due to the increase in the number of companies and technological development, new requirements will emerge and these requirements will bring along different teams and formations.

Communication is the center of every field and scope and it is the most important focus of them. Communication is supremely important and its importance is increasingly growing. Access to communication is easy and it spreads to the world quickly. Communication is not just a concept or issue, it is a resource. It is a very extensive, detailed and deep resource. That's why, in the past, today and in the future, communication is among the most important requirements and principles within the frame of management understanding.

Nowadays, communication, mediation, shopping and everything have been adapted to virtual environment and it facilitates our access. These developments lead to an increase in the need for virtual teams.

Technology enables us to provide communication in different locations irrespective of time and distance. At this point, internet / virtual environment / technology, however you call, these resources open the door of the world in a very short time regardless of the distance. As a result, for the formation of teams, especially for the ones in different locations, it is not necessary for them to be in the same location and to work in the same environment or place. When you provide communication, others would be additional reasons. Therefore, virtual teams can easily be established.

Common point of virtual teams is same within the frame of management principles and management scopes. The difference is moving requirements, management and team principles to the virtual environment. The principles that I will mention will be sufficient for you to cope with this issue. Adaptation and the new leadership issues shed light on this issue particularly. Additional requirements of virtual teams actually are not different from effective leadership requirements. Making good use of technology, being dominant, applying the principles of team management, preventing shattering and retaining control. For you not seeing your team and for your team not seeing you actually should not bring together loafing and irregularity psychologically. You should find the necessary method to avoid these problems.

You may encounter new team systems and different leadership understandings and you definitely will do. Please note that they all have the same common point. In the future, there will be new revolutionary tendencies which change the current leadership understanding such as new leadership and new team system. However do not be fooled! Today's basic principles are the principles which will always be able to protect and renew themselves. Moving away from these principles does not bring a new perspective. That will completely change the leadership understanding and make the leadership serve other people's purposes. I take it as my duty to give advance warning. Remember these lines when you face with such situations in the future.

Leadership in the Art and Art Management

Art has been existed since the past and continues to shed light on the future. Art is distinguished from many fields since it constantly produces, exhibits variability, knows no bounds and develops. Art, which is one of the basic building blocks of culture is included in our lives either in a voluntary or involuntary way. Even everyone is not occupied with art in-depth, by listening to music, occasionally going to cinema and theater or at least watching television they are involved in art in a voluntary or involuntary manner. Escaping from art is unlikely. Yet, moving away from art and not involving in art means being away from productivity, different forms of expression, and activities and functions in this regard.

For leaders art is important,since it expresses a wide range from reflections of individual and multiple criticisms to explanandums and multiple situations. Perspective and management of leader who is involved in art and has a grasp of it are one step ahead of the other leaders'. For that reason, leaders who are artists and have a grasp of art are within the scope of effective leadership.

As for art management is form of management that requires full domination on all fields of art and effort to increase efficiency in matters about art and artist. Nowadays perspectives to art management firstly focus on commercial structure and financial gain instead of artistic value. Of course every art manager does not have the same understanding and we see individual differences and hence these differences highlight specific artists in this regard.

As well as these art manager combines political situation, financial situation, the structure of artist, artistic merit and motivation at a common denominator and brings out a new approach which is different from conventional management approach.

Respect, Dignity

Word meaning of respect describes value and reverence owing to this value and respect exists in all areas of our lives. Some people shape their relations and environment according to respect, but according to some of them respect is something trivial or not necessary.

Respect is not a concept that is shown someone. Respect can be shown to a work done, living or non-living thing or anything else. On the other hand, dignity is the respect that the individual has gained. However this is a formation which is based on specific foundations different from others and shapes in line with dignity concept. Dignity forms depending upon environment, people, rules and principles.

We may consider respect in two ways:

1. Respect which is shown wishfully: It is the respect shown voluntarily.

2. Respect which is shown due to position: It is the understanding that shows respect to a person as a necessity due to his title, position or dignity.

First one is a preference, but second one is a requirement.

Examples to the second one are typically such as respect shown to prime minister or president. At this point, regardless of the position, there might be people who say that showing or not showing respect is my own decision. Here, there are two understandings namely principle based or freedom based.

<u>Principle Based:</u> About this understanding, let's go through the example about prime minister and president. Here penalties that vary with respect to laws and countries emerge at this point.

In return of the disrespect to president and realizing this disrespectful behavior there will be a punishment for it.

<u>Freedom Based:</u> Difference of the freedom based understanding from the principle based one is it puts forward freedom. That is to say, it gives everyone the freedom of showing or not showing respect and leaves this choice to individuals.

These two understanding models cover the basics which extend from the past to the future. Right or wrong is not applicable for them. They vary from person to person and from country to country. As well as these if we handle the relationship of respect with leadership, respect and dignity are two of the foundations of leadership. Effective leaders are dignified leaders. Effective leaders are respected, it is necessary to show respect to them.

Leadership is an expression that requires respect regardless of the position. A leader who does not have dignity cannot be an effective leader either. Of course, everyone does not have to show respect. However, effective leaders are respected people in general.

Dignity affects you in many scopes from the power to have something done to the relationship with people you are leading. At this point, using the dignity properly and losing it are also indications of effective leadership.

Love, Value

Love is the total of feeling, emotion, quality and concept that lead people to pay close attention and commitment to any subject, scope, or person.

Can you imagine a life devoid of love? How can you live a life without love? Is love something you need? Does the meaning of love change every day? Do people become ungrateful as they are deprive of love? What is the definition of love for you? Do you feel lack of love? How do you evaluate the relationship of people around you with love? What can lack of love lead to? What can excess of love lead to?

After a short questioning ask these questions to yourself and to those around you periodically. Also, you can derive new questions. Periodically questioning yourself in the sense of love will enable you to take steps in the way of being an effective individual and then an effective leader ...

Value is a concept that we encounter in many respects. Mathematics, social sciences, law and in many other areas it is used. In fact they are associated with each other regardless of their usage areas. Its meaning in our daily lives is the meaning that we have ascribed to a subject, scope or person such as our cultural values, our personal values etc. At this point, the scope of the value is very wide. Like love, it can be associated with every topic, scope or person.

What is the value for you? Are you a valuable person? Do you see yourself as valuable? Do you value yourself? Do you value your environment? Do people value each other? Do animals value each other? Do living things value each other? Is it rational to value non-living things? Do we protect our values? Do we appreciate our values? What are the things that are valuable for you? What is your most important value? What is your least important value? Is value an issue that should exist and be cared about?

In this book we deal with many issues about leadership, management and administration. Each subject and scope are really valuable. We have dealt with many issues, but being deprived of love and value in both our lives and management area will reduce the impact of all of these issues and also make most of them ineffective. So, without these two concepts, your life would be shaped seriously. You would not be able to apply the concepts not only in this book, but also in many other books and you will feel the deficiency. Being full of love and value always keeps you one step ahead. Obviously, this is strategy as well. The distinction between these two is people who act strategically in terms of love and value live struggle in themselves but they live peace at outside.However people who live love and value actually bring positiveness for both themselves and their environment. Is not it the time to hit the road just before your love and values become blunt? Come on, it is time to hit the road ...

Intuitive Leadership

We cannot make logical decisions and take logical steps continuously. Sometimes we may need to decide quickly or we may decide as we feel like instead of thinking before decision.

So, what is in us that manages us? Can we control our intuition? Can we improve them?

Intuition is not one of the basic principles of leadership but certainly it has a significant place for many of the leaders. Intuitive leadership reveals the decision making process with intuition, but this should not be a leadership only based on intuition. Intuition is part of the leadership and this qualification, it is not the whole and also it should not be. Intuition may vary from person to person, thus some leaders may shape their intuition, some enter into the domination of their intuition, some do not pay attention to their intuition, some bring their intuition into the forefront and make them decision center.

In fact, when we look at it, there is no good or bad, right or wrong. It may vary according to your leadership, your leadership understanding, your unique character and personality. Here the important basic principle is that intuition positively influence your leadership and your decisions. If it influences you and your decisions adversely and misleads you, then you should think about it and take the action.

Being a leader is both easy and difficult, isn't it?

Classroom Management

Teachers, academics, professors, in short everyone in education. In particular, classroom management is a topic within your scope.

We know that teachers are mentors, some of them are coach-esque leaders and some of them show leadership qualities. The greatest difference between non-leader teacher and leader teacher is the gain and perspective differences in students. Coach-esque leader is close to the concept of mentor but it can be used to define instructive and guiding structure of teacher.

Collecting the attention of students during education, directing, teaching something directly or indirectly are within the structure of classroom management. Teachers who perform classroom management well exhibit leader quality. Managing classroom is not as easy as it is assumed. Consequently, every teacher cannot manage classroom or may remain incapable of managing it. Classroom management is not to be applied with intense discipline. Realization of management is more important than ensuring effective classroom management. Teachers have various attention gathering and teaching methods. Teachers who have unique systems can also act within the boundaries of creative leadership.

Abstract and Concrete Leadership Concepts

Abstract means concepts that can be undetectable by senses, concrete means concepts that can be detectable by senses.

First of all, leadership is an abstract concept. Leadership is not something that can be tangible and perceivable. It is a comment open to discussion. The effect of leadership is concrete. Its results, activities, traces, power to influence are concrete concepts. At this point I prefer to define leadership as both abstract and concrete concept.

Leadership in Sport

Sport is an essential part of healthy living. As life cannot continue without health, healthy life concept would be deficient without sport.

Sport is carried out in different areas, in different formats and with different abilities. While at individual sports, individual effort and individual trainers exist; at team sports, individual effort, team effort and both individual and team trainers exist.

At individual sports, as a result of self-improvement efforts, sportsman become his own leader in the first stage. In addition to this, coach and other trainers lead that sportsman.

At the individual sports, main objective of the trainer is the sportsman that he trains. This training is one individual focused and centered.

At team sports, sportsman continues his efforts in two basic aspects: the individual and the team. Firstly he undertakes his own leadership then he undertakes the leadership of the team or he harmonize with the leader in the team. At team sports, coaches are both individual and team oriented or individual trainers and team coach are designed separately but team coach should take the lead and work both individual-oriented and team-oriented. The selected player in the team becomes captain and the leader of other players and this cause an increase in the activation of the coach. In this sense, the captain is the leader and responsible for both himself and the team as well. He conducts motivation, organization, discipline and quality-enhancing activities within the team and push the team to forefront not himself. A captain who has these qualifications is an effective captain and has leadership quality. With his relations not only inside the field, but also outside the field he takes the lead of his team and highlights the union.

So, is everyone who does sports sportsman? Everyone who does sport is not sportsman. Being sportsman is realized on the basis of certain principles and discipline. Being a sportsman becomes meaningful with exemplary qualities, behaviors and attitudes. In this context, we can observe that it is consistent with leadership again.

So, is every sportsman a leader? Every sportsman is a leader. If we go back to the beginning, every sportsman is the leader of himself. Of course, there are steps of leadership and in this sense the leadership level of the sportsman depends on the sportsman himself and his qualifications. Every sportsman exhibit exemplary attitudes for individuals at different circumstances and fields. Consequently, sportsmen are leaders.

Strategic Thinking

Strategy is not a concept that is applied substantially only in management. It is a part of thoughts and the intellectual leadership. For this reason, at many events in our lives, we apply some sort of strategies in our own way. In many resources, you can observe the steps of strategy and its types with regard to the topics covered. But I'll stand on the basic logic and focus of the strategy. Because the strategy starts in the brain and application of this strategy occurs thanks to the brain.

If we touch briefly to the formation of the strategy, it can be expressed as variations of all factors in your life, your environment and in your influence field.

According to my definition, "What you want to do, your target, and the way you choose are also strategies." At this point your choices in the way you trace are strategies as well.

Many things that you need to pay attention about the strategy are the same as in the context of effective leadership. For example, being creative, determining priorities, taking the team and the environment into consideration, being dynamic etc.

So, in all activities done and in all steps taken is there a strategy? Of course, there are people, leaders and managers in defiance of the strategy. Additionally, since strategy has savior and efficiency enhancing function, when strategy is implemented, efficiency enhancement, prevention of waste of time, reaching to the target will be at stake.

At the implementation stage of the strategy we can use apply-see or try-see concepts. They are as follows:

<u>Apply-see:</u> It refers to observation the application of the strategy that you created, seeing the results, taking positive and negative lessons.

<u>Try-see:</u> It refers to taking precaution or making certain of events that will develop under the effect of the strategy by means of simulations, small experiments and observations.

In parallel with the crisis management, preparation / pre-plan can be qualified as try-see within the scope of this topic. Whatever the consistency and accuracy of your strategy is, to try, to think of the consequences, to argue the scopes within its environment and impact will be among the chief factors in eliminating the drawbacks during the developing process.

Continuity

Continuity refers to an understanding that continues and repeats at regular intervals. Permanent continuity is only for machines. Rather, we can apply flawed and partial continuity. Because living conditions, more importantly, our nature presents uniqueness and distinctness. At this point we need to go through the continuity that we have provided and achieved.

Continuity is an important principle in leadership, management, success, and attaining efficiency. This is because, a uniform and non-repetitive understanding brings along a de facto and non-persistent understanding. Of course, even a striking move will not be permanent if it does not have repetitive and continuous feature.

Luck

Are you lucky in your life? Is there anyone that you call as very lucky in your neighborhood? So, at which rate does it affect your life? Do you believe in luck? Do you think working hard is enough to achieve success? Using a fixed definition or statement on this issue would be wrong. The reason is that luck may be different for everyone. Therefore, some people act only on the basis of it and some act by ignoring it ...

Leaders or managers that we define as lucky, are lucky or successful? Or are they both lucky and successful? I leave this topic to you. However you should not only focus on luck and also you should not act by only relying on your chance because effective leadership requires this.

Do you believe in bad luck? Do you have any superstitions? Do you have people around you who believe in them? Do you think it is rational? Can it be controlled? Or is advanced stage of it a disease? Sometimes we say that some people have the luck of the devil. This is a significant nature that is conspicuous and outstanding. Whether you call it the luck of the devil or anything else, as a leader you must be always in the foreground, obvious and clear. Whether or not you have luck, you should create chances for yourself, your team and your surroundings, you should create new opportunities and be an exemplary leader.

Chief

Chief is a borrowed word in Turkish. As word meaning chief is the person who manages, has the authority and the responsibility, leads and has director position. It is a qualification that we encounter in many areas. To give examples of the use of the chief at certain areas: At music, chief of the orchestra; at meal, chief of the waiters or in the sense of cooking food chef; at transportation station chief; at work bureau chief are some of these examples.

Essentially chief is the person who has little or large responsibility and takes place at the head of a community to manage them. At many field and scope, being chief is possible. For this, experience, qualification and practice are required.

Let's reinforce our narrative about food management. From the selected material to the presentation, taste, staff relations, timing, and coordination issues chief becomes prominent and important. Chief is the leader and mentor of that environment and those people.

You may not have great success in your life. However, do you think that you have struggled enough? We see that leadership is at everywhere ... If you are cook why should not you be a chef cook, if you are a waiter why should not you be chief waiter, if you are a cleaner, why should not you be a chief cleaner? Why should not you strive to improve yourself? What will you lose? Everyone wants to be rich, everyone wants to be senior manager. However facts show that there are very few people who succeed. Why should not you take place among these very few people? Let's say you cannot achieve it, then why should not you be the leader of your own world? Are being leader of your own business, your own family and your own not enough for you?

Being Watchdog

We're watching many things in our lives either by being aware or being unaware of them. These affect our preferences, decisions, orientations directly or indirectly. When we follow in commercial terms, our financial tendencies change in that way. Besides when we follow within the frame of our lives, people that we follow and take as example influence us.

Things that we follow are actually people that we take as example or interests that we have passion for. At this point whatever we follow affect us and our preferences.

Effective leaders follow things that constitute example for themselves, they follow negativities from which they will take lesson, effective leaders follow and they are followed by many people.

Imitation

We face imitating usually within the frame of humor. Whereas, good imitation has different effects in each area. For example in basketball, players who are good at imitation makes fake moves and weaken defensive players and perform their shot. Likewise you can make other person see himself by imitating him ...

When imitation is applied skillfully it turns into art, when it is applied unprofessionally it turns into comedy and when it is applied for taking example it turns into wannabe.

Imitation gains qualification according to its scope. In the field of leadership there is not exact imitation. There is the synthesis of the imitation of those which are taken as example and the integration of this synthesis with yourself. That is because, a simple imitation is just doing something similar to an existing one. This situation is completely contrary to creativity. Here different from creativity, producing something by taking example and adding something from yourself is in question. At this point, leaders are not people far from creativity. So, at which level of leadership are they?

In particular, in effective leadership this synthesis is achieved supremely. While in radical leadership sharp changes exist, in imitator leadership a new synthesized product is at stake. Again in this sense, it is clear that a complete imitation understanding is far from the upper stages of the leadership and administration.

Style

Anyone can be leaders in different places,but everyone cannot be a permanent leader or manager. In order to be permanent, success, effectiveness or authenticity are the required features. Without possessing at least one of these three features, being permanent is not possible. I believe that, particularly important concept in permanence is the authenticity. Of course, different ideas can be put forward but permanence cannot remain limited to authenticity only. However, authenticity brings about difference, and difference brings about contradiction with the usual activities and putting forward a new issue. In brief, sum of them is the style. I would prefer to express the definition of style in this way. If briefly stated, style is the unique circumstances of an individual. In this context, style is important in the leadership and administratorship. In fact, same type of leaders are steadily declining today.

Style of the leader and manager can be observed in many ways. In appearance, wording, mode, preferred methods, strategies and many applications style is available. Making a particular style specific to you is beyond most people's depth. Leaders and managers who assimilate into that approach will get very different yield at each step or way he has taken.

Style is also important in terms of charming feature. Charismatic leadership plays a key role in persuasive skill. In this context, we can say that we face style in communication. From the appearance to the preferred wording, we can mention style. As well as these, of course we cannot say that every style owner leader will be successful or will be an effective leader. In every effective leader, style is not among the key features. At this point, this issue is up to the choice of the leaders and managers. So, what do you think about style and in what aspects style is important? Do you own style?

Technology Management

Technology is an important issue that is constantly evolving and affecting our lives (also its influence is gradually increasing). As you will notice I did not say concept. Because it cannot be restrained to a concept. It is also an important issue.

In management system, adaptation to the environment, domination on the environment, utilization of materials and ideas exist. Especially utilization of the materials has impact on your time. We will face these materials especially technological ones within the scope of environment and surrounding.

Nowadays, people who does not know how to use computers, does not use smart phone, so to speak people ignorant of the technology, do not have the chance to take part in management level, it is almost an impossible situation. This situation unfolds the promotion of technology from being a requirement to being an obligation. Especially in the field of business and competitive environment, technology and computer usage are not only an advantage but also become a provision almost at every higher education institution.

As well as these, technology management becomes an increasingly difficult case. The classical question that asks whether technology administers us or vice versa, brings together many questions.

Technology can make or break a leader. Today, there are many companies systems and accounts of which have been taken over by hackers. At this point, it would not be wrong to say that importance of technology management has gradually increased within the principles of management.

Meeting Management

Meeting is the foremost requirement of the business life, the inevitable arms of the management approach and the main source of management skill.

Meeting is the collection of more than one person for any purpose. Of course, we will focus on its relationship with the management approach. When meeting is conducted effectively it may turn into a real success or it may lead to wrong outcomes. This is primarily related with how the meeting is conducted, what the scope of the meeting, is and with whom the meeting was made.

How is the effective meeting realized?

First, classic, well-known, and standard meeting approach has already been put aside. Of course this does not mean that in the future this approach will not be applied again, but today and in the near future meeting approach has started to move away from the classical, well-known, and standard meeting approach. At this point the impact of the world, country, groups, individuals, objectives, goals, technology is at stake.

Standard, Well-known, Classical Meeting Approach

- Serious people
- Formal clothes
- Hours of talks

Current and Near Future Meeting Approach

- Optional seriousness
- Optional formal, semi-formal, informal clothes
- Brief talks as far as possible

In general, the main issue that I want to focus on is the basic principles in a meeting and being effective rather than the meeting approach. Effectiveness is common, it does not change.

<u>Effective Meeting:</u>

- Determine and know the purpose of the meeting.
- Estimate your expectations from the meeting and the results of the meeting.
- Determine and know the people who will participate in the meeting in accordance with the scope.
- Start the meeting at the specified time, finish in the specified time.
- Determine the meeting agenda, do not go beyond the agenda as possible.
- Get everyone's opinion, pay attention to the ideas.
- Listen to each other.
- Avoid distracting behaviors.

Meeting Types:

Board Meeting: It is the meeting of a board which is held on any particular context.

Coordination Meeting: It is the meeting to ensure coordination between units.

Commission Meeting: it is the meeting held by experts of a specific subject about that subject.

Appointment Meeting: It is the meeting based on sharing and assigning tasks to people.

Informative meeting: It is the meeting for informational purposes to give information about any topic.

Opinion Meeting: It is the meeting based on the exchange of ideas, views, and information.

Problem Detection Meeting: It is the meeting based on determination of the adverse situation and problem.

Problem Solving Meeting: It is the meeting based on problem solving, finding solutions, finding methods, and result oriented working.

Principle Meeting: It is the meeting which is held in order to define the principles, gain principles and present rules and system.

Recognition Meeting: It is the meeting to enable people to know each other, to provide togetherness of the team, to ensure recognition between different units and teams which are gathered together for any purpose.

Status Review Meeting: It is the meeting to assess the current situation.

<u>Result Review Meeting:</u> It is the meeting to evaluate the results, review what has been done and prepare the basis for the actions to be taken.

As well as these, preferred seating arrangement during the meeting, discourse materials, comfort level are among the factors that will affect the course of the meeting.

You may encounter many different characters during the meeting. These characters may exhibit behaviors that may disrupt the meeting or may impair your calmness. Meanwhile, during the meeting, exhibit your performance at the same level without compromising yourself, your decisions, and your thoughts.

Conformance

As we live we continuously face with different situations and different people at different environments. In the meantime, ensure compliance is not always an easy task. Sometimes we are forced to do, sometimes we do not dwell on it. Under the circumstances, harmony and conformance are inevitable topics in most areas of our lives.

Everyone does not have to conform with everything. Also everything is not has to be compatible with everyone. However, at critical moments in our lives we may need to be harmonious and conformant. At this point, necessarily we act in a framework willingly or unwillingly, conformably or unconformably. It is a changing move according to the case, people, initiative and decision.

When we move leadership based, we face with the same consequences within the frame of the same subject. However the most important element that discriminates effective leader from others is his ability to comply with anywhere, anything, any situation and any person easily. That is why, effective leaders do not have compliance problems or they tackle with the problems that they live. Effective leaders live both a busy and a modest life. They are constantly in a changing pace and accumulation. Especially in this context, they are effective on entering-exiting different environments, having conformance with contacts, adapting and making the environment to adapt.

Managing Your Superior

Let us examine this issue in two ways:

- Pursuit of individual for the self interest
- Pursuit of individual for the company and the team

Let me explain why I have started to this topic by making such a division. Usually people do not mention the fact that the concept and principles of managing your superior is a political game or it is about the pursuit of an individual for his self-interest. Perhaps because it stems from good intention or they are contrary attitudes to the principles of effective leadership. For this reason, I prefer to explain this subject within two scopes,since there are two separate manager concepts about this subject today. Let's look at these two concepts:

<u>Pursuit of individual for the self-interest</u>: People who care about their career, want to promote, have stars in their eyes are always trying to manage their superiors in line with their self-interests. They are in effort to uncover their superiors' fraud or try to get closer to their superiors. We encounter people who accomplish this goal by using different ways. Demand for promotion, improvement and

climbing the steps of leadership and administratorship are natural desires, of course. However, an understanding which focuses on only benefits is unfortunately far away from leadership. Let me remind you again that, leaders do not only consider their own interests or their own responsibility, they also consider other factors, their team and people around them. Therefore, it is necessary to separate personal interests from developmental effort.

Pursuit of individual for the company and the team: Managing and knowing your superior will enable your team and company to develop more efficiently and quickly. Knowing your boss or your manager and his demands will bring along preparation in advance and conducting effective work to reach a solution. By this way your team, your company, your superior, and you will have the ability to move fast.

Of course, managing your superior is not as easy as managing your subordinate. Of course, it may vary between individuals but to a very large extent it is like that. It is not an easy task as assumed, because of the goal to implement this on someone who manages you. At the end of the day, he is the one who can either fire or promote you.

Within the scope of this issue, we must distinguish two statements from one another. These are,

Individual, targets efficiency by continuously working within the frame of team and company.

Individual, goes beyond his superior and ensures the dominance within the company and concomitantly rules his superior in real terms.

The first expression is already stable. Exact definition of managing your superior is the second statement. Looking at the second statement,

- It can be said that individual is an effective leader. In order to manage your superior,
- Know your and your manager's strengths, weaknesses, goals, working style and needs.
- Establishing an open communication brings along openness between parties.
- Give place to activities which unites you and your manager at a common denominator.
- Make your manager to feel even partially that he is your superior. Express him what you can do for him.
- Go to your manager's office with studies and information which are similar or same to the style that he wants.
- Be honest, reliable and understandable.
- Do not waste your manager's, your team's and your time unnecessarily.
- Put forth double-sided expectations clearly.
- Present ideas, be creative.
- Do not slip leadership and administration of your team through your fingers.
- Be entrepreneur.

- Control and develop your subordinates and units, developed.

- Maintain your own progress, do not lose your dynamism.

- If you want to object to any issue or if you have found a mistake, express it in a peaceful manner with examples (proving) and without blaming.

- Do not engage in tasks that you cannot do.

- In essence be an effective leader.

Yield Management

Yield is a continuity obtained in any activity. Yield can be expressed in the form of both continuous and discontinuous. The reason why I have expressed continuity in the definition of the yield is as well as continuity has result feature, it may take place in the process and yield occurs as a result of this process. Yield may occur after a particular part of the process or in the middle or in the result. This depends on the structure of the yield. However yield does not occur at the beginning of the process. This reveals the relationship between yield and process.

The structure of the yield varies depending on the scope of the subject, external and internal factors, and the individual. Yield management covers the entire yield process and it is a solution-oriented approach. In order to consider yield management as successful, it will be enough to obtain a yield more or less. Importance of the overall process is dependent on the result-based studies.

Yield is important. For any subject, obtaining yield at any level is important. This yield may be material or spiritual, in practice or in theory, it does not matter. At this point, what matters is the gain. Enabling the effectiveness of yield is realized by gains. Contribution of an individual to himself and his environment,is when you obtain a tangible yield , will be corporative gain, when you obtain a spiritual yield again, will be an environmental, structural and personal gain and so these are criteria of yield indicator. When yield management gains continuity and is applied effectively, it opens the door of success. Of course, in the meantime, management skills and personal dedication are important. Being result-oriented is the basic application to do so as to benefit from the yield at the end of the process.

Vision

Vision shows where a company wants to be in the future. This definition complies with the management-administratorship relations in particular. In general, vision is the image in which you see yourself in the future. Vision also has a direct impact on people's lives. A vision holder person sees the effects of it in every area of his life. In this context, we can say that vision is one of the success factors. If we examine the vision in the scope of management we can divide it into two, as personal and team:

<u>Personal Vision:</u> It refers to the vision of individual and can be described as the images in individual's mind.

<u>Team Vision:</u> It refers to the vision of the whole team. Likewise, it can be described as common images in team's mind.

The aforementioned images are concepts and connotations that we have created in our minds.

Vision is not for today, it is for tomorrow. It is not just for the future, but for tomorrow which also covers today. It is a concept that is revealed in the light of today's scope.

If we look at the relationship between the vision and the leadership,we see every leader is not a vision holder. Vision holder leaders are also called visionary leaders. Visionary leaders take place within the scope of effective leadership, because it takes the advantage of the leadership language to create tomorrow by covering today as well. The way to design the future also brings along accidents. Therefore, it is important to have a vision.

Creativity Management

As it can be understood from the root of the word, creativity is to create to unearth. We encounter this concept in many areas. Is creativity a talent or is it something that can be improved?

When I define creativity, I highlight that creativity is an ability and also it can be improved. Because talent is the one that exists, revealing this one is the skill. Talent cannot be put into practice without skill. If it is put into practice, it does not make sense and reveals an unproved character at its surrounding. Advertising, social media, science, technology and creativity which play a very important role in today's world are directly related to creativity and being well-equipped. Being creative and producing new ideas and projects require changing the ordinary way for leaders and managers. Creativity management refers to the management of the skills that I have just expressed.

Every creative person cannot perform the creativity management. People who perform both are undoubtedly leaders. At this point, people who are creative but does not have dominance on creativity management should get help from people who are dominant on this management and so they can obtain an effective product.

Motivation in Our Lives

While time passes away against us and while there is a process which constantly evolving, changing, and diminishing against us, what are we doing, what should we do and do we know what we are doing?

Throughout our lives, we face with many obstacles, difficulties, hardship, negativity and sometimes we are not happy with that or we do not want to do anything or we cannot get yield from what we do. In the meantime, so as to get yield from the work, you should increase your own efficiency and determine your priority on an individual basis. In this context assess your motivation and motivate yourself.

How can you motivate yourself and how can you maintain your motivation? I will explain a three steps method which is short and easy to apply in order to help you to uncover your motivation and maintain it.

1. <u>Knowing yourself:</u> Get to know yourself. Physically, mentally, logically, and virtually identify your potential, things you have done, things you can do, things you want to do and things you do not want to do.

Briefly get to know yourself completely. In particular within the scope of fomentation, what are the things that motivate us or what should we do or what should we have in order to motivate ourselves? Question these questions to yourself and then answer them.

2. <u>Focus on Motivation-Clear Negativities:</u> Always have the thoughts in your mind that motivate yourself. Do not let the negativities and disable them at a certain extent.

3. <u>Orient to the Result:</u> Attain the motivation and the goal that you have defined for yourself. This result does not matter whether it is tangible, intangible, spiritual, practical, logical or emotional. Learn to motivate yourself and get the consequences. Do not forget that people who do not motivate themselves, mostly affected by adversities and cannot overcome the obstacles would experience difficulties and move away from success.

Stress in Our Lives

In our constantly changing life which has ups and downs, positivities and negativities stress is inevitable. Some have less, some have more and some have sickly level of stress. So, are you a stressful one? Are you aware of yourself? This is because, not everyone may admit stress, they can deny. Management issues accompany stress. However, leaders, teams and managers who provide an opening to stress now and in the future are less successful than others. Stress precludes activities and reduces productivity. In basic principles there exists a calm, thoughtful, unhurried understanding.

So, what do you do when you realize that you are stressed? You can ask yourself the following questions, for example:

- Why I'm stressed, what is the basis (source) of my stress? (Get to know your stress)
- How can I do away with my stress? (Overcome your stress)

- Have I overcome my stress? Why could I overcome it?/ Did not I overcome my stress? Why did not I overcome? (Question, know yourself and diagnose)

- If I do these again (...) stress will not knock my door again. (Take lesson and take precaution)

In general, these questions are for recognizing stress, controlling it and finding a solution to it. The one who can overcome the individual's stress is the individual himself. What are your ways to get rid of stress? Discover your own way and if you have one apply now and see the results. Before it beats you hit the road ...

Competition in Our Lives

In today's world and our lives, competition has become an inevitable case. In all areas, at all levels and everywhere competition exists. Of course, this situation brings with many consequences. Continuous competitive environment makes people more aggressive, more brutal, and worse. Whereas, people who knows competition well, understands it and turns it into advantage are tolerant and warm-hearted people. These people mentioned above are rare and usually they are effective leaders.

If we examine competition under different titles, it can be classified under six titles.

1. Competition of the individual with himself: The greatest competition is the competition between your own potential and your current performance. The greatest measure for an individual is himself. Leader who is constantly in competition with himself develops himself consistently and struggles to produce better performance. In the meantime, what should be considered is not to rush into extremes. If the continuous competition is healthy,

it will give positive results. Uncontrolled competition is not a competition and is not healthy.

2. Competition with other individuals: Individuals have the potential to enter into competition with other people in the environment that they are involved. Competition is often inevitable. In the meantime, you have to be fair, not compromise yourself and not forsake truths by avoiding the greed of competition.

3. Competition between teams: Competition between teams is a holistic competition approach. Instead of competition between individuals, it explains the performance of the team, the performance of the counter team and the competition of these teams' performance. Of course, every competition is not based on performance. Any subject that is based on knowledge, experience, equipment and people are suitable for competition.

4. Competition between units: To give example on the basis of a company, competition between different units of a company is called competition between units.

5. Competition between companies: It is the most known competition type. It describes the rivalry and race between companies.

6. Competition between managers: Competition between managers has various types such as title namely position competition, performance competition, success competition, knowledge competition;

material and spiritual competition and so on. As well as these, effective leader is the leader who turns this competition into his advantage. Not to make concession to your principles and yourself should be your priority and meantime you should be careful that you have been given your due and also you have given someone else's due.

Being a New Manager

I am not talking about being a new leader because leadership brings along newness and innovation and requires adaptation to this innovation. We have mentioned that in the scope of developmental leadership and effective leadership. Different from these, there exists a preferred constantly renewing understanding in management and administration areas and it is almost impossible to escape from the innovation in these areas.

Being new is not creating something that does not exist or changing something that is old. It may have those meanings but every newness about your life such as entering a new environment, change of job, change of city, change of country are actually in this context. Renewing your room, your desk, your behavior, even your pen has the power to change and renew your life.

To be the new manager can be expressed in this regard. To mention about administratorship, changing mission and vision of the company that you manage are examples of radical changes of administratorship and they have serious importance for being a new manager.

Being a new manager will be in some way refreshing yourself. For you, it will conduce to gain a different point of view, obtain different results and reviews. Either mandatorily or non-mandatorily, being a new manager is a significant improvement in your life. Also in mandatory changes, it will be the best move to change misery to happiness and disadvantage to advantage. This is in your hands. Do not forget that time is very precious and carry your ideas into effect as immediate as possible. Nevertheless, it is your choice.

Talent Management

In today's world where change occurs very fast, organizations have begun to realize that talented employees enable them to create difference by means of new and creative ideas on the way towards success and their objectives. And these organizations try to retain their talented employees and utilize them ideally. Today's and future's management system focuses on individual-based development, talent and equipment.

Basic factors such as talent, education, internal and external environment, self-devotion fall into the scope of individual-based development and it shapes in accordance with these factors. In talent management, as well as being talented, managing that talent effectively is also very important,since talent is an owned concept. Talent management is a form of management that reveals, implements, develops and reinforces talent. For this reason, when talented people cannot manage their talent, they will waste it and at the same time talented people who do not engage in talent management but aware of it should apply talent management by the help of a consultant, advisor or someone who is expert in this regard.

Talented people and people who are engaged in talent management come into prominence in leadership and realizing the potential and they become more permanent.

Authority

Power or authority. It is the ability and capacity to establish dominance, gain confidence and provide obedience about any topic or scope. Although authority has a close meaning to dignity, it refers to being expert in a specific area. In both scopes authority has importance about leadership, management and administratorship issues. If we address them in general;

Leaders must have the authority and establish authority over people and groups. Management is a topic of authority in itself. Especially those working in this field, wise people, leaders, managers and consultants are required to have authority.

Authorization Competence

In leadership, management and administration task sharing and task arrangement are of paramount importance. A leader or manager who is in the upper level is not the omniscient one, he is the one who shares duties and scopes between the people who will do them best. Not everyone knows everything because of everyone's nature, their structure, talents, abilities and interests are different. Therefore, knowing them well and doing the task sharing in line with this scope is the things that an effective leader can do. Authorization competence is directly to manager and leader. Meanwhile communication, behavior and wording are very important in general. As wording is shaped in a better way, authorization level rises as well. As well as these, after doing necessary authorizations, applying and tracking their application are equally important. People whom you authorize can be the best in the area but maybe they cannot apply or other results may arise. At that time application and tracking come in sight. Authorization competence not only covers the authorization. It covers the entire process, prior to authorization, during authorization and after authorization.

Mentor

Mentor is a concept that we encounter in leadership scope. It means referring, directing. Leadership covers mentorship, but mentorship doesn't cover leadership.. Mentorship is one of the qualities and principles of leadership. Another confused concept is leadership. Leader means leading and pioneering but mentoring means directing and reorienting. All mentors are not leaders and all leaders are not mentors. Mentorship can be improved and should be improved. Today, even senior leaders and managers have mentors, people or entities that give direction to them.

Steps of Administratorship

The steps of administratorship can be expressed in different ways.I prefer to express in five steps. If we look at these steps,

1. Fixed Manager
2. Professional Manager
3. Areal Manager
4. Leader and Manager
5. Effective Leader and Manager

1. Fixed Manager: Is the manager restricted to small circles, institutions and areas.
2. Professional Manager: Is the manager of people and organizations by his profession or by his assignment and has a limited management capability.
3. Areal Manager: Is the manager who can manage his location and surrounding area, have a grasp of management concept and have cross-domain knowledge and experience.

4. Leader and Manager: Although these two concepts are separate ones, they are close to each other. An individual who has both of these will have lost of experience and have an understanding to be dominant on leadership and administratorship steps.

5. Effective Leader and Manager: It is the administratorship understanding which is specialized on leadership and administratorship, be able to manage all types of organizations, activities, environments and people, is professional, has knowledge and experience, and has full dominance on leadership/administratorship.

Although the first two steps of the administratorship are within the scope of monotonic and particular understanding, without them, management steps cannot be climbed up. Different from these two leadership steps, third, fourth and fifth steps however, are associated with leadership steps which are climbed up one by one. However, unlike the leadership, administratorship cannot proceed without experience and application. Even it goes forward, this will be limited to a certain step. In our constantly evolving and developing world, it is impossible to know and dominate everything. Therefore, for managers one of the important features in administratorship is taking opinion from or working with someone who knows the subject better than the manager and acting according to that. Controlling this varies in line with the quality for the third, fourth and fifth steps.

Management Systems

Management systems mean systematization of the management, a management understanding based on system or division of management understanding and philosophy into specific areas. Every management understanding doesn't rely on system, there is no obligation about this. However at almost all of the current management understandings, management is carried out in a systematic way. Although ideological backgrounds are different and there are different opinions, common denominator is that both of them have systems. A completely independent and unsystematic leadership, management or administratorship understanding is not at stake and it would be confined to marginality. Even such an initiative is applied, this would be a different and new understanding which is realized apart from leadership, management and administratorship. There are many reasons for the systematization of management. Above all, a systematic scheme leads to less time loss. Self-ordained behaviors will be eliminated or reduced and also tasks and results are evident. What are the reasons for systematization of management, what do you think about it?

Governance

Unlike the management term, governance is the management style based on bureaucratic structure. Although this definition is used in general, it can appear in different areas and scopes. Because governance is a word that may correspond to the unification of management and interaction or management and communication words. The governance concept takes place around a specific bureaucratic environment. This environment is not constant, it varies. This is realized with country based systems such as constitutional order, regime and traditions. Leaders who are under the scope of governance are classified according to their governance steps. These steps are different from leadership and administration steps. By means of hierarchical configuration, within the frame of management science, these steps are carried out. In this regard, the president can be exemplified as the upmost of these steps. As this can vary depending on the country, in some countries president is located at the top of this structure and in some of them prime minister is located at the top. Thus, officials in the lower and middle levels are formed according to the structure.

Superficiality and Profundity

Not only in management philosophy and system, in our daily lives about which subjects and scopes we think and apply superficial, in which ones we think and apply in depth?

Superficiality is the part remaining on the water without going into detail. Profundity is all of the water together with details. In management understanding and principles of leadership and administratorship, neither superficiality nor profundity is true. This point is important and it is often confused. In some issues we may stick to the principle of superficiality and in some issues we may stick to the principle of profundity. However if the general understanding is based on superficiality or profundity for exceptional issues, an orientation which has digressed away from the system would have occurred and its results would not be estimated.

Profundity may seem as omniscience and a completely holistic dominance but this is actually a big mistake. The wise saying, "success is in the details" might be the right expression for success, but this is not the case for management and leadership issues. Excessive profundity brings along quick distractibility, loss of time, unqualifiedness of people and decrease of efficiency. On the other hand, excessive superficiality brings along failure and unqualifiedness. At this point ensuring stability is necessary. So, how is this balance achieved? If we approach in terms of superficiality and profundity examples, while superficiality is the surface of water, profundity is the entire water. The balance between them is the amount of water taken by ladle. That is the amount which is taken from both of these approaches at a certain extent and at a sufficient level.

Leadership in Time and Time Management

Undoubtedly, time is a concept that manages our lives and we form our lives according to it. In fact, time manages us. As we don't have the chance to stop, to forward or to rewind time, time manages us. During this management, we must value, use and form our time according to ourselves. In fact we define the measurement system for the time. In this context, clock is one of the means for measuring time. Instead of measuring time, we can say that it is a tool that shows the course of time or by means of it we can express time in a suitable way. Within the frame of this tool, we see the slices in our lives and execute plans and programs in this context. Time is very important for leaders and managers. As well as making good use of time, efficient distribution of time is important. Managers and leaders who use time in an unbalanced way cannot obtain success completely, because time of the success is one of the most important building blocks of it. Consequently, a success which is obtained late does not have importance and value. What is important is the success realized timely and in the most efficient manner. In our daily lives and in our plans, we are using the time and we are the ones doing the time distribution. Each individual forms his own time and act accordingly. People who do not actualize time distribution well are constantly faced with problem in their business and private lives.

Timing

Effective leaders do the right thing at the right time, do the necessary thing when necessary. Timing is doing or not doing something in time. While timings which are made at different times are called timing error, realizing the necessary condition when necessary is called synchronization. In this matter, necessary time is a relative concept and as well, in the leadership perspective many foundations are same and unchangeable, they are not relative too. At this point, timing is considered as doing necessary thing when necessary for the effective leaders. In another aspect, the success can be described as doing the right thing at the right time. This expression is open to discussion. However in the general sense, the effect of making good timing on people is an important issue.

Epilogue

We have dealt with many areas, scopes, concepts and qualifications. Reading until this section by showing patience; is also an indication of placing value and importance to yourself and your environment. As well as these, your desire to improve yourself in leadership, management and administratorship areas and to add additional value to your knowledge and qualification will push you one step forward in the leadership and administratorship ladder. I wish that I have done albeit a little favor for your life. I pay my best wishes and regards .

Aybars Öztuna

He was born in Ankara on May 1, 1999. He completed his primary and secondary education in the Yüce College. In Bahçeşehir University he was the youngest participant of the Government and Leadership School. He took International Affairs courses in Sabancı University. He had Urban Design course by participating in British Columbia University Future Global Leaders team. Currently, he has been continuing his high school education in Canada Bodwell High School & Academy. He has good command of Turkish , English and German.

Between the years 2007-2010, he was interested in Aikido and attained brown belt. From the year 2010 to 2012, he played in BOA Sports Club and Yüce Schools. Between 2012-2016, he played as a point guard and captain in Ankara Private Yüce Sport Club and Private Yüce Schools. In 2013 he joined Galatasaray Basketball Camp. During NBA Camp 2014, he was named best camper. Currently he has been playing in Vancouver Bruins Basketball Team.

He undertook the duty of School Assembly Secretary in 2010, School Assembly Permanent Membership and Radio Club Presidency in 2011, Middle School Presidency, Ankara District Student Assembly Membership, Discipline Board Membership, Debating Jury Presidency, Social Assistance and Solidarity Club Presidency, Events Board Membership, Science Festival Jury Presidency in 2012, School Assembly Permanent Membership in 2013, Advisor of the President of the High School in 2014, High School Presidency, Culture and Literature Publication Club Presidency, Council Board Presidency, Turkey Active System Founder, Media Department Presidency, School Newspaper Editorship, YCMUN founding member and Finance and Logistics Director, World's Youngest Writer in Politics in 2015.

In 2016, he has undertaken the duty of Young Leaders Association Founder and Chairman of the Board and World's Youngest Author about Business Strategy & Terminology , Unity House Captain , Student Parliamentary Prime Minister.

In 2012 he began to songwriting, composition and recorded his demos. In 2014 he was the founder of Turkey's youngest rock band "Canis Majoris" became the lead guitarist. In 2015, he released "Restoration" album. In 2016 he released his second album, "Orc-Extra". Aybars Oztuna set up his orchestra in 2017 and assumed maestro duty.

He worked for various Non-Governmental Organizations. He has given lectures about subjects in which he is expert.

He wrote essays on music, politics and sports. His books translated different languages and sold in many countries.

He is the author of these books ;

- To Be Light ToThe Politicians
- Leadership Management Administratorship
- To Remember Yılmaz Öztuna
- Have A Career On Age Of 16

CPSIA information can be obtained
at www.ICGtesting.com
Printed in the USA
LVOW08s0604130117
520850LV00001B/1/P